CONTEXTS OF UNDERSTANDING

Pragmatics & Beyond

An Interdisciplinary Series of Language Studies

No. 6

Herman Parret

Contexts of Understanding

CONTEXTS OF UNDERSTANDING

HERMAN PARRET
Belgian National Science Foundation

AMSTERDAM / JOHN BENJAMINS B.V.

1980

PREFACE

Significance and Understanding (Chapter 2.) has been published
before in *Dialectica* 33(1979): 3/4, 297-318, and *Perspectival Understanding* (Chapter 3.) in H. Parret and J. Bouveresse (eds.), *Meaning
and Understanding* (Berlin/New York: Walter de Gruyter Verlag, 1980).
Parts of the *Introduction* (Chapter 1.) have already been used and elaborated in the Introduction to the *Meaning and Understanding* volume,
jointly written by J. Bouveresse and myself. *Contextualism and Transcendentalism in the Theory of Understanding* (Chapter 4.) was never published before.

An earlier version of *Significance and Understanding* was read at
the *Third International Conference on the Philosophy of Language* at
Biel (Switzerland), May 1978. Versions of all chapters of this book
have been presented at the Philosophy Departments of the Universities
of Warwick, Birmingham, Tel Aviv, California (Berkeley), and of the
Wolfgang-Goethe Universität at Frankfurt. Endless discussions with
helpful friends have clarified the content and the style of my thought:
I am especially indebted to Karl-Otto Apel, Jerry Bruner, Arnold Burms,
Wim de Pater, Marc de Rouck, Urbain Dhondt, Susan Haack, Luise Hoiker-
Hardy, David Holdcroft, Francis Jacques, Manny Schegloff, Julius Morav-
csik, Stephen Schiffer, Pierre Swiggers and Ivar Tonisson.

I wish to thank the Philosophy Department at Stanford University
where I was in residence in 1977 and in 1978 when I was first writing

on aspects of the theory of understanding. Most of the writing has been done at the Netherlands Institute for Advanced Study (N.I.A.S.), Wassenaar (The Netherlands), whose hospitality enabled me to set up this book.

H.P.
June 1980

TABLE OF CONTENTS

vii

1. INTRODUCTION

1.1 *The difficulty of understanding understanding*

Understanding is evidently difficult to understand[1]. Understanding
itself being one of the objects that we can or wish to understand, we
may ask why we spontaneously place it at such a high level on the scale
of the difficulty of understanding. It is relatively easy to explain
why a mathematical demonstration, a work of art, a human being or a
historical event can be more difficult to understand than other objects
of understanding. However, does the fact that understanding differs
from one type of object to another, mean that there is no common meas-
ure allowing us to appreciate the difficulty of understanding something
in general ? Compare the questions "How can understanding be achieved ?"
and "How can one win a game ?". Although we recognize that there is no
general and uniform answer to the latter (valid *a priori* for all games),
this still will not lead us to the idea that winning is especially difficult to understand. However, this is the type of answer required for
the former question: the various "activities" that we call *to understand*
should show, as a result of their being, a kind of unity related to the
exercise of one and the same faculty. But, if we are prepared to admit
that there are as many ways of understanding as there are ways of winning a game, we should also admit that the difficulty of understanding
understanding has nothing to do with the impossibility of satisfactorily
answering the question of what understanding *is*, considered as performance and achievement of one and the same specific type.

Can we understand understanding ? Is a "theory of understanding"
possible ? Let me first suggest why it is so difficult to understand

understanding, and why a "theory of understanding" is so unlikely to
be achieved or to be adequate. There are, indeed, several possible
reasons for the resistance of understanding to understanding. It may
be that understanding is particularly difficult to analyse or to explain because of its *complexity*; or the problem may reside in the ab-
solute *singularity*, and hence *simplicity*, of its character; or the
resistance of understanding to understanding can result from the fact
that understanding is an essentially *fuzzy concept*.

Let me say a word on the idea that understanding as an object of
understanding is a vague, indistinct and fuzzy concept. It is evident
that, in this last case, it is in vain to strive for retrieval by reconstructing criteria of application that constitute necessary and
sufficient conditions for saying, in a general way, that someone understands something. To understand understanding would be impossible
because it would appear impossible to explain, or to analyse, or to
elucidate the concept of understanding: those, like Popper, who consider that there is no real explanation, nor an 'explained' or even
'precise' concept, will admit that our effort to understand does not
have to go beyond the prevention of non-understanding (i.e. in our
case: non-understanding understanding) in as far as it is predictable,
and prejudicial to the solution of true problems.

Others, like Ziff[2], are more optimistic: they claim that understanding will be understood by way of an analytic procedure whose difficulty is related to the structural *complexity* of the object concerned. But this argument is applied counterintuitively to understanding
itself as so-called 'complex' object of understanding: one has the intuition that understanding understanding is more a problem of *synthesis*
than of analysis. Moreover, it is not clear, for instance in the case
of the understanding of sentences, that the most difficult to understand is always the most complex. It seems beyond doubt that understanding understanding is not obstructed by the peculiar complexity
but by the *'singularity'* of the object of understanding.

This singularity may originate in its exceptional and unlikely
properties, *or* in its extremely common, mundane and familiar character.

It may be that understanding should be understood by *Selbstverständ-lichkeit*. A classical example in this respect, discussed by Wittgenstein, is the question Augustine poses in relation to *time*: our ignorance here is not based on an insufficient experience but on the fact that it concerns aspects of our understanding which are *too close* to us and too evident for us. Time *is already* understood, just as understanding is *already understood* before we explain or elucidate it[3].

In some cases, I agree, explanation provides us with an effective understanding that we lacked previously; but, in other cases, explanation shows us simply *that* and *why* we understood already. And, if there are, as suggested by Augustine and Wittgenstein, fundamental objects that we understand without being able to explain them, then it should not be surprising that understanding should be one of them. Indeed, it suffices to look at the classical view of 'philosophical understanding': philosophy should be the wondering about what grows from itself, and thus the generation of a certain type of 'non-understanding' of objects that seem to be the best understood. In this sense, philosophical understanding, just as psychoanalysis, according to Kraus, is the disease of which it regards itself as the cure. The difference between scientific and philosophical wondering then could be that in philosophy we should try to understand in another mode the objects that we *already* understand in a certain way, whereas in science we should endeavour to explain objects we do not really understand at the outset. If we consider Augustine's way of handling the matter of time, we could say, by analogy, that the difficulty of understanding understanding originates not so much in lacking an adequate explanation of something the discovery of which should probably be a long-winded enterprise, but rather in its *Selbstverständlichkeit*, or in the fact that understanding, in fact, *is* already understood.

1.2 Understanding versus explanation, interpretation and translation

"In order to *understand*, I have to be able to *explain*" is a slogan which is fairly common in the philosophy of science: the Explana-

tion/Understanding Controversy[4] concerns precisely the adequacy of
this equation. Taking as the paradigm of understanding in this essay
the understanding of natural language fragments, I can easily abstract
from this controversy: the equation of understanding and explanation
is totally inadequate when the object of understanding is meaning-in-
language. Other equations have to be taken more seriously:"The more
I know, the better I understand", "The better I interpret, the better
I understand". I will have to come back to the Knowledge/Understanding
relation, which is an essential aspect of the theoretical proposals I
make myself[5]. Let me say a few words, in this introduction, on the Un-
derstanding/Interpretation relation (and especially on the theory considering interpretation as a process of translation).

     Roughly speaking one could say that neither continental philosophy
nor   analytical philosphy stress the centrality of a theory of understanding. Continental philosophy, especially hermeneutics (in the Ger-
man-French philosphical climate), argues that the theory of *interpretation is* a theory of understanding, whereas anglosaxon philosophy suggests that the theory of *meaning is* a theory of understanding. Understanding is somehow an intermediate concept, reduced either to interpretation or to meaning. There is indeed some reason to say, like Apel
does[6], that *"understanding* makes up a broad field of possible meeting
and mutual illumination of hermeneutics and analytical philosophy".
Both theories of interpretation and of meaning finally could meet as a
theory of understanding. This would be concordant with the more general
trend of reconciliation between two traditions: the hermeneutic tradition, definitely delivered from psychologism, and the analytic tradition, leaving more and more the reconstruction of a model of the ideal
language to the trend of a pragmatic approach to natural language, will
meet inevitably and unconditionally. However, one should not be too
optimistic, for instance with regard to the integration of the theories
of interpretation and of meaning. The initiation of a dialogue between
the two tendencies should not conceal the fact that hermeneutics has
always in the past appreciatively evaluated a type of understanding

that, even today, is still unconsidered by its rival: the primary concern of hermeneutics was not the *communicative* understanding of the texts by contemporaries, but rather how the meaning of the texts could be understood by people of a later epoch by way of their *historical* understanding. What interested classical hermeneutics thus is not ordinary understanding within a given linguistic and conceptual community, but rather understanding 'of a second order' of an understanding that is not accessible except by the bias of historical research. More generally, hermeneutics pays specific attention to the type of understanding that seems to require a sort of 'auto-transcendence' of our own faculty of understanding, intrinsically delimited by the context of the *language game* that we are effectuating and by the context of the 'form of life' in which we participate. If the reconciliation of hermeneutics and analytical philosophy should be pursued - for instance, through an *integrated* theory of understanding - one should remain aware of two problems, one with respect to hermeneutics, the other with respect to analytical philosophy.

The first problem, indeed, is that of the precise appreciation of the intuitions of hermeneutics - let us take Heidegger and Gadamer as examples - with regard to the intrinsically temporal and historical character of significance, while at the same time avoiding the traps of neo-historicism, of relativism and of scepticism threatening any hermeneutical theory that leaves the regulative and normative view of meaning and truth. A 'regulative idea' (à la Kant) of possible progress in hermeneutical truth, as Apel calls it[/], should be reintroduced in hermeneutics in one form or another. We know too well, at this point, that the tendency to rehabilitate prejudice and tradition in general as preconditions of understanding prevents hermeneutics - for instance, in Gadamer's *Truth and Method*[8] - from devoting sufficient attention to a prejudice that plays a crucial role in a normative-critical understanding of texts and permits evaluation of their truth claim, namely the *ideal norm* of possible true knowledge of the object of understanding. The second problem then, with regard to analytical philosophy,

has to do with the fact that one of the most fertile, but at the same
time most controversial methodological abstractions of analytical philosophy, even in its pragmatic and intentionalist version, is to have
put in parentheses the *historical* dimension of meaning and to have ignored the quasi-communication and quasi-dialogue between different
periods. This quasi-communication and quasi-dialogue cannot but be
understood in the perspective of the progressive realisation of an
argumentative community of universal understanding, to which all participants in an empirically-determined cultural and linguistic community implicitly address themselves. This means that any speech act
is historically conditioned, implying at the same time a constitutive
interest in transcending the limits of its own historicity and in
reaching a future audience extensible in time and space in an unre-
stricted way.

Let us suppose, for a moment, that a solution for these two problems is found; can we say, then, that the theory of interpretation *is*
a theory of understanding ? Let us suppose, for instance, that the
historical dimension is built in within meaning and significance - on
the side of analytical philosophy -, and that a *normative* concept of
meaning and truth is accepted - on the side of hermeneutics. Even with
these fundamental, yet hypothetical corrections, it would still be the
case that the problem of understanding, in the properly hermeneutical
sense of the term, would remain that of an 'exegetic' process resolv-
ing difficulties of understanding or even absence of understanding.
Contemporary hermeneutics cannot resist the temptation to purely and
simply *identify* understanding and interpretation, or not to recognise
a difference in nature, not only in degree, between the understanding
of a language one speaks and the interpretation of a foreign language.
Yet, as McDowell notes[9], "A good *interpretation* of a foreign language
would equip its possessor to put a construction on what he hears, in
such a way as to arrive at a position which cognitively matches that
of those who *simply understand* utterances in the language. But the
difference is essential". Moreover, the hermeneutical idea that all

inter- or intralinguistic communication equals *translation*, as it is
worked out, for instance, by George Steiner[10], should be radically
excluded. To generalise the hermeneutical concepts of interpretation
and translation to all cases of understanding goes together with a
more or less clear tendency to accord to immediate and ordinary understanding the status of authentic understanding. Instead of equating
understanding and interpretation, it is certainly more reasonable to
consider, like Wittgenstein did, the concept of interpretation as nor-
mally correlated with that of a *plurality* of possible interpretations:
there is a plurality of interpretations for one and the same understanding. It is only when we take a *reflexive* attitude towards it that
understanding can be seen to be composed in all cases of a more or less
hypothetical 'interpretation' of acoustic or graphic materials that
we perceive immediately.

Even if we should accept that ordinary understanding of a sentence
is an 'interpretation' obtained by the unconscious application of semantic (and possibly pragmatic) rules, this certainly does not mean that
there is any reason to declare that all understanding results from and
is equal to an interpretation. Just as the hermeneutical concept of
translation is relevant only in cases where a precise translation is
not immediately available, the concept of *interpretation* does not ap-
ply to cases where interpretation results automatically from understanding the language, where 'understanding the language' can be char-
acterised by a systematic theory or even through the faculty of a common communicative competence as far as this faculty is described as
implicit knowledge of a system of determined rules.

It has been rather fashionable in this respect to present Wittgenstein as an angular stone where hermeneutical and analytical philosophy meet, for instance around the notion of understanding *as* interpretation. I strongly oppose that view because of some respect for
Wittgenstein's specificity. One word may be sufficient here. It proves
inadequate to characterise the opposition between Wittgenstein's view
and that of Gadamer as a prototype of hermeneutics, *only* as one of a

static theory versus a dynamic theory of language games. It is precisely the autonomy of grammar, and the onforeseeability of language games
depending on it, that *prevents* Wittgenstein from adopting a historico-
transcendental perspective. It has been suggested[11] that the historicity of language games should be understood as corresponding to a universal language game of human history, of which the community of understanding and 'dialogue' realised by philosophers through the ages already constitutes a tangible anticipation. However, Wittgenstein tends
to conceive of the historicity of language games as a direct expression of the *absence* of their foundation and as the manifestation of
their resistance to reflexive philosophical ambitions, rather than as
the privileged dimension in which the problem of the foundation or the
justification should find its solution through the process of the ex-
emplary 'language game', which the history of philosophy is. This ex-
emplariness of philosophical discourse with regard to ordinary linguistic activity, and of philosophical understanding with regard to
usual understanding, is the first bias *denounced* (rightly or wrongly)
by Wittgenstein. In fact, I do not read anything in Wittgenstein which
would indicate that understanding *is* interpretation, hence that the
theory of interpretation should serve *as* a theory of understanding.

1.3 *Aspects of a psycho-pragmatic theory of understanding*

As I would like to make clear (especially in Chapter 4. of this
book), Wittgenstein, indeed, is the starting point of my argument.
Wittgenstein taught us so convincingly in the *Logical Investigations*
that understanding is neither explanation nor interpretation, and
neither an experience nor a mental state. Understanding is an *ability*:
a person who understands something is able to do certain things. This
ability to understand, as I will argue, is *extrinsic*: even if one says
in a Wittgensteinian manner that understanding is performing by the
use of rules, it should be clear that this is not a purely psychological operation, internal to the speaker/understander, but an operation-
in-the-world. One understands when one is 'practically' related to the

poles of the triangle: the speaker, the expression and mundane fragments. My stress on so-called *contextualism* is, in fact, a consequence
of the extrinsic character of the ability of understanding. This will
have as a direct side-effect my reaction against all attempts to identify the (semantic or Fregean) theory of meaning with the theory of
understanding, or, in other words, the reconstruction of a theory of
meaning *as* a theory of understanding. Thus at the starting point,
understanding is *doubly* pragmatically oriented: *as an ability*, and as
essentially related to *contexts* of all kinds. Contexts can 'prolifer-
ate', indeed, in the theory of understanding.

Why, then, call the inchoative theory presented here, a *psycho-*
pragmatic theory of understanding ? As Wittgenstein, I do not consider
understanding to be a mental state nor an immanent operation. Psychologism, in general, should be attacked at any place where it alienates
a philosophical problem by neglecting the autonomous linguistic and
socio-conventional characteristics of phenomena. Yet the theory of
understanding is *psycho*-pragmatic because constellations of psychological primitives are aspects of *what* and *how* we understand, although
these constellations are necessarily *constrained* by a *Describability
Principle* (see Chapter 2.), which has an essential link with the lin-
guisticity and the socio-conventionality of what and how we understand.
We cannot abstract from the functional role of psychological primitives: indeed, they are operations on contents, although they are themselves dominated by more powerful operators which are not psychological
at all and which are openly given in public language use within a normative community. The introduction, on a very specific and circumscribed
level, of psychological primitives is less anti-Wittgensteinian than
it seems at first sight, as I evidently would like my readers to believe.

The necessity of *pragmatic transcendentalia* (see Chapter 4.2.)
in the theory of understanding will be argued for, although a parsimony
principle should stop their proliferation (in contrast to the salutary
multiplicity of contexts). We all know Wittgenstein's criticism of

transcendentalism, and, again, I go a long way with Wittgenstein in his condemnation of obscure transcendental powers. Still, there is a kind of transcendentalia one cannot avoid in order to escape relativism, but - in contradistinction with convinced exponents of 'transcendental language pragmatics', like Habermas and Apel - one should be parsimonious by restraining transcendental principles and by interpreting them in a narrow Kantian way. The *contextualistic* and *transcendentalist* perspectives on understanding are, in the end, enriching the Wittgensteinian starting point. They allow for a well-balanced theory of understanding, of which some aspects are inchoatively and modestly presented in this book.

2. SIGNIFICANCE AND UNDERSTANDING

We speak of understanding a sentence, an argument, a proof, a road indication, a joke, a work of art. We understand a person, a purpose, an intention, an event. We do not speak of understanding a stone, but rather the molecular structure of the stone; we do not speak of understanding a mountain, but the mountains as they are represented in Cezanne's paintings. To understand is to have a relation with a *value*: molecular structures and artistic representations are values of cultural activities such as science and art. This is why understanding cannot be explained in naturalistic or purely 'objectivistic' terms. To understand, in fact, is to understand human values - the values of the individual, the values of the community - through one or another semiotic expression: *signs* always are intersubjective mediations. It has often been said, in the hermeneutical and even in the analytical tradition, that understanding has a non-propositional component. Understanding transcends mere 'grasping' of the propositional content of the sentence, the argument, the proof, the road indication, the joke, the work of art: one understands once one 'knows' about the anthropological conditions governing the production of sentences, arguments, proofs, road indications, jokes and works of art, and these conditions are non-propositional because they are rooted in the internal structure of the participants of semiotic processes; these participants are men, creators of significance, with their idiosyncratic but also general and basic needs, intentions and purposes. This philosophical position, with its anthropological orientation, is the inspiration for the theory of understanding inchoately developed here, and a starting point once the technicalities have to be elaborated.

Thus, the focus will be on *what* we understand when we are said
to understand semiotic sequences, such as sentences, arguments, proofs,
road indications, jokes, and works of art, and on *how* we can understand
them. My contention is that we always understand *significances,* and
that we can understand significances by the fact that they are *descriptively presented* to the users of semiotic systems *as common values*
of the community to which they belong and want to belong.

Elaborating the central notion of significance and its relation
to the notion of descriptive mode of presentation within an overall
theory of understanding, I rely heavily on current discussions between
what I consider to be the three paradigmatic theories of meaning of
our days: the theory of meaning as a truth theory (exemplified most
plausible way in Davidson's work), the theory of meaning as an 'assertability condition' - theory (in Michael Dummett's neo-fregean framework), and the theory of meaning as an intentional theory (along the
lines of Grice). Violating the traditional terminology, I prefer 'significance'[12] to 'meaning', and a 'theory of signifying' to a 'theory
of meaning'. Theories of meaning, in the classical sense, reconstruct
the meaning of semiotic strings as abstract objects without taking
into account the fact that these objects are the results of *signifying
as an activity*. Care has to be taken to insure that a theory of meaning
transcends mere descriptiveness in order to become a fully explanatory
theory of signifying. I consider that understanding has to be given a
psycho-pragmatic base; a *semantic* theory claiming to explain understanding cannot be but the preparation for the development of psycho-
pragmatic theory of the significance of semiotic strings and of the
attitudes of the participants in semiotic processes. Nevertheless, I
wish to stress immediately that psychological reductionism - and
psychologism, in general - has to be banned by means of a strong constraint which will appear to be an epistemological one. Psychologism
is a powerful, alienating philosophical machine, and the philosopher
has to escape it by being conscious, among others, of the social fac-

tor involved in any process of understanding.

2.1 Acceptance

Understanding is a relation between a person or a subject S and
a value v. It is almost always implicitly admitted that understanding
is, within the communicative scheme, an 'activity' of the addressee;
the speaker *produces* the sequence and the interlocutor *understands* it.
Rules of production and rules of understanding or reception are totally
different according to the classical directional scheme. However, this
is not the option I would like to defend. On the contrary, I consider
the theory of communicative behavior to be *non-directional*, the locutor being as much 'listener' as the interlocutor, and the interlocutor being as 'active' as the locutor[13]. Both locutor and interlocutor have a relation of *acceptance* with the significance realised by a
semiotic string, and this very primacy of the acceptance relation
renders the distinction between the status of the locutor and of the
interlocutor rather marginal. *Understanding* is *signifying*, and the
subject S (either the locutor or the interlocutor) signifies when understanding, and understands when signifying. The subject's propositional attitude when signifying is that of acceptance, and the object
of acceptance is a value, not a truth value but a desirable justificatory value for his signifying.

To signify is to *infer* from a *sequence* to a *significance*. Three
notions have to be explained here: inference, sequence and significance.

(1) I am aware of the risks of using the term 'practical inference' instead of 'pragmatic inference'. Usually, 'practical' syllogisms
and 'practical' inferences are said to have actions *as their conclu-
sions*. Within the framework I am defending practical reasoning, practical syllogisms and practical inferences have to be considered to be
actions - intentional actions - *themselves* of which the conclusion then
is a value or a significance[14]. I do not take an explicit stand against
or in favor of the thesis of the autonomy of practical reasoning[15]; I
prefer to escape the choice by saying that the relation between theo-

retical (or alethic) reasoning and practical reasoning can be formulated as a *validation* relation: theoretical reasoning, as I read Kant,
has to be validated by fundamental practical laws, at work in practical reasoning, and not the opposite as is maintained by logicistic
epistemologists[16].

(2) The *sequence* from which a significance is 'practically inferred' is a semiotic string; in fact, linguistic utterances are proto-
types of semiotic expressions - therefore, the notation of a semiotic
sequence can be U(tterance). A sequence U is a pragma-syntactic structure; it is a grammatical entity with a *given* or immanent meaning.
Still, I call this string a *pragma*-syntactic structure because of the
fact that the syntactic distribution is accounted for by a derivational
history (generative semanticists should say a *trans*derivational history) originating in the 'stereotypical' context. This stereotypical
context is not the *factual* context of utterance but the grammatically
reconstructed context, to be presupposed by an adequate theory of syntactic distribution. I know the difficulties, treated in the metho-
dology of linguistics, concerning the status of a pragmatically motivated syntax: this, however, cannot be my concern here, as I am here
more interested in the structure of the inferred significance of the
semiotic string than in a theory of the 'given' or immanent meaning
of the pragma-syntactic distribution of this string.

(3) Inferred from the semiotic sequence U is the acceptance value
ACC(v). To signify is to infer practically ACC(v) from U. The acceptance of v by S has two basic aspects or forms: *D-acceptance* (desire-
acceptance or *wanting*, and *J-acceptance* or *judging*. This distinction
is made on the basis of the anthropological insight that wanting and
judging are the essential categories characterizing men's practical
and theoretical reason[17]. The centrality of these categories constitutes the link between the theory of significance and its philosophical
infrastructure. ACC(v) is, in fact, ACC[D-J](v).

2.2 What we understand when understanding

ACC[D-J](v), in propositional terms, is to be identified with η[φ(p)].

The proposition p is modified by two operators: an operator with universal scope, called π, and an operator with partial scope, called φ. The η-operator (to be translated, in approximate common sense terms, by "One can reasonably conclude that ...", "the reasonable conclusion is that ...") has the function of indicating that the significance of the sequence can be considered as the conclusion of a valid argument of practical reasoning (or as the conclusion of a 'practical syllogism'): the π-operator indicates the general *rationality* of the significance determined by the fact that the significance of the sequence is derived by rules of practical inference. The π-operator functions as the partial modifier of the radical p: it indicates the *mood* of the significance. Moods are distinct from grammatical modes (indicative, imperative, interrogative) as well as from the basic speech acts where the typology is radically dependent on the existence of conventional means (performative verbs, for example); the typology of moods of semiotic (or linguistic) strings, on the contrary, is a matter of specific combinations of the two psychological primitives, wanting and judging.

The sequence U has a significance π[φ(p)] and, therefore, signifies ACC [D-J](v) or a value which is acceptable for the psychological structure (the wanting-judging) of the subject S, if and only if (1) the propositional component p of the significance is modified by the mood-operator $φ_1$, $φ_2$, ...$φ_n$, according to the *local* attitude of acceptance by S, and (2)[φ(p)] itself is modified by the rationality-operator π, according to the *essential* attitude of acceptance by S. I concentrate in this section on the essential attitude of S which is the universal basis of all meaningful language functioning (and broader, of any meaningful semiotic process).

When can[φ(p)] be said to be *rational* ? When can one "*reasonably* conclude that [φ(p)] " ? The essential attitude of acceptance of S gets

two main explanations in the literature, but only the second approach
seems to me to be adequate. (a.) According to the *epistemic* interpretation of rationality, S signifies by inferring $\pi[\varphi(p)]$ from U if S *be-*
lieves the supplementation of the transition from U to $[\varphi(p)]$ to be a
valid argument. (b.) According to the *intentional* interpretation of
rationality, S signifies by inferring $\pi[\varphi(p)]$ from U if S *intends* the supplementation of the transition from U to $[\varphi(p)]$ to be a valid argument.
The position taken in this dispute has direct consequences. I defend
the thesis that the rationality of $[\varphi(p)]$ is dependent of *what S intends*
(of which the nature will be specified later on), and not on what he
believes: the validity of the argument *has to be intended*, not to be
believed[18]. The epistemic interpretation of rationality claims that
$[\varphi(p)]$ is rational, which means that $[\varphi(p)]$ can be considered $\pi[\varphi(p)]$,
if the inference from the sequence to the significance is *believed* by
S to be valid. This interpretation cannot be adequate for major reasons
originating in the anthropological foundation of the theory of significance and understanding. I mention two of the most compelling ones.
The claim that the rationality of $[\varphi(p)]$ is dependent on S's belief
in the validity of the inference, necessarily leads to a *solipsistic*
and *static* conception of rationality. This conception turns out to be
solipsistic because S's belief in the validity of the inference originates in the internal structure of his mental states, especially
the set of already present beliefs, without the necessity of being
sanctioned by any intersubjective evaluation: rationality, in this
case, cannot be disproved by counterarguments from outside. Rationality, however, is intersubjective, not solipsistic, and therefore it
cannot be given a purely epistemic characterization. As I oppose the
intersubjective to the solipsistic conception of rationality, I oppose
the *active* to the static conception too. Rationality being defined in
terms of beliefs, one cannot even grasp anymore why the practical inference from the sequence to the significance is an *action*: epistemic
states modify and amend other epistemic states without externalization
and without any 'practical' consequences, such as new cultural events

in science, art and ordinary life, or such as creative interhuman relations. Of course, solipsism and stasis are side effects of one and
the same paradigm of explanation: mentalism, with its 'perverse' notion
of (algorithmic) creativity and of the 'inner life of the mind', as
opposed to intersubjective creativity and to human interactions in the
world.

What exactly, then, does it mean that the rationality of $[\varphi(p)]$
is dependent on what S intends, and more precisely on S's intention
that the supplementation of the transition from U to $[\varphi(p)]$ should be
a valid argument ? S *intends* the validity of the inference in a very
specific sense. S intends the inference to be valid, if and only if
he *wants* $[\varphi(p)]$ to be *judged*. The rationality of $[\varphi(p)]$ is radically
dependent of the essential attitude of *acceptance* by S. The intentional
interpretation of rationality claims that $[\varphi(p)]$ is a significance, a
$\pi[\varphi(p)]$, if S *accepts* the value v, which means that he wants
to be judged. There are no intermediate beliefs, there is no intentionality outside the essential combination of the two psychological primitives, wanting and judging. To intend the validity of an argument, to
be *rational* such that the conclusion of the argument becomes rational
(in other words, such that $[\varphi(p)]$ becomes $\pi[\varphi(p)]$, is to *want* $[\varphi(p)]$
to be *judged*. Two more amendments have to be added immediately render-
ing my thesis clear and coherent: they concern the question of *who*
judges and *what* exactly will be judged when S wants $[\varphi(p)]$ to be
judged.

Who judges $[\varphi(p)]$? Let X be the audience; X can be a factual interlocutor, a hypothetic class of addressees (the readers of a literary
work, the drivers interpreting road indications), a socially delimited
group, or, in its maximal extension, the community of rational beings
manifesting meaningful semiotic and linguistic behavior. S, *intending*
his argument to be valid, *wants* X to *judge* $[\varphi(p)]$. The audience X
judges $[\varphi(p)]$, and this is what S wants and admits as a condition
for his own rationality. Even when there are circumstances in which
S himself judges $[\varphi(p)]$ and wants $[\varphi(p)]$ to be judged by himself, ra-

tionality will require that his judgment *substitutes* X's judging, and,
therefore, can be contested, affirmed or suspended. X - and eventually
S as substitute for X, thus X[S] - judges [φ(p)] and this is what S wants
when rational.

What will be judged when S wants [φ (p)]to be judged by X[S] ?
X[S] judges the *desirability* of[φ (p)];this, however, cannot be the
desirability of[φ (p)] either for S or for X, but it has to be the *common desirability* or S-X desirability (desirability for S *and* X). This
is the only way to escape psychological circularity where S would want
the audience to judge if [φ (p)] is desirable for S *himself*. There is
no communication and no rational semiotic behavior possible without a
criterion of generality:[φ (p)] has to be judged by X[S] with the standards of the S-X community (the community of which S and X are members), i.e. [φ (p)] is a common value and, therefore, judged by X[S] to
be desirable for S-X. What makes [φ (p)] desirable is a controversial
point in philosophical psychology, and speculations on what makes an
object a *desirable* object or a value leads us away from the theory of
significance itself[19].

Thus, the significance π[φ(p)] can be translated as "It is rational
that [φ (p)]", or "S intends the validity of the inference of [φ (p)]",
or "S wants [φ(p)] to be judged by X[S]". Consider as an example the
sentence "You are a great composer" of which the indicative is the
grammatical mode, assertion the speech act type, and the judicative
the *mood* φ: in fact,[φ(p)] is "I judge that you are a great composer".
The sentence "Be a great composer" has a volitive mood, being an order
(speech act (type) and an imperative (grammatical mode):[φ(p)] here is
"I desire (I want) that you be a great composer". To avoid additional
problems I suggest that both sentences carry the same propositional
content, the radical p. The overall significance of our judicative
sentence is "S wants that X[S] judges that S judges that you are a
great composer" where X and *you* can be identified. The overall significance of our volitive sentence will be "S wants that X[S] judges
that S wants (or desires) that you are a great composer" where X and

you can be identified. The overall significance of our volitive sentence will be "S wants that X[S] judges that S wants (or desires) that you are a great composer" where X and *you*, again, can be identified[20]. My thesis being that *understanding a semiotic sequence* is to understand its *significance*, understanding our judicative sentence will be to *understand its* $\pi[\varphi(p)]$, namely: "S wants that X[S] judges that S judges that you are a great composer". Let me clarify further what precisely is understood by the locutor S when he signifies (*produces* the significance) $\pi[\varphi(p)]$: "I want that you judge that I judge that you are a great composer"; the interlocutor X or *you*, *'receiving'* the significance $\pi[\varphi(p)]$, understands: "You want that I judge that you judge that I am a great composer" where *you*, of course, has to be identified with the locutor S. Other judicatives, such as "Bach is a great composer" (a construction with a third person subject and without deictic markers), "Your wife is drunk" (where φ contains the special modality that, finally, *you* judge p, and that, according to π, I want that you judge φ), "Water is H_2O" (natural kind definition of which the subject is a 'rigid designator'[21]), have significances which are structured in a similar way; this can also be said of types of volitives other than the type "Be a great composer", and, in general, of all sentences. Of course, classification and typologies are necessary because, even when the π-component is universal, the φ-component remains specific[22] and the radical p particular to each sentence itself.

If this is *what* we understand when we are said to understand a *sentence*, we still have to extend the thesis to the understanding of other types of semiotic sequences, such as arguments, proofs, road indications, jokes and works of art. There is no space here to work out, even inchoately, a description of the significance of these semiotic strings. But, in principle, *understanding* these sequences is understanding their significance $\pi[\varphi(p)]$. The subject S is an extensive notion, just like the notion of an audience X was: S may be embodied as a person but the subjectivity at work in the π- and the φ-component may also be person-*neutral*, such as the Authority (the politico-administrative authority in the case of road regulations, the authority of

'experts' in the case of arguments and proofs), and even undefinable
(when a work of art *invites* for interpretation, S or the subjectivity
who 'invites' is, of course, not the artist, but Art itself in its marginal existence). The popular metaphor according to which understanding
is "to accept an invitation (S's wanting) by interpretation (X's judging)" shows clearly what is at work when understanding a semiotic sequence. Diversification within the overall theory of understanding, in
order to explain *types* of understanding of *types* of significances, may
be rendered possible by thorough exploration of various constitutive
factors. (1) The *pragma-syntactic structure of the sequence*: U is linguistic (joke), non-linguistic (road indication) or para-linguistic
(work of art); U is sentential (sentence, road indication) or macro-
sentential (joke, proof); U is 'simple' (the immanent meaning is the
meaning of *the form*, in all examples except the work of art) or 'complex' (the meaning is the meaning of the form, colors and pictorial
structures, and *of the substance*, the landscape or the represented
object, in figurative painting at least). (2) *Types of S's intention*
which make the inference of the significance valid: S may have an open
or hidden intention; his intention can be suspended or weakened, without abolishing, however, the interpretability of S's intention *and its
deviances*. (3) The *rationality-operator* π, within the significance,
being universal, will be affected nevertheless by the *specificity of
S and X*. The sentence "You are a great composer" has a person-bound S
and X, deictically manifested and understood as intrinsic elements of
the π-component, whereas the significance of the work of art has a
rationality where the subjectivity of S and X is person-neutral. Proofs,
in scientific literature, may have an intermediate position on this
axis. Another source of diversification within the π-component is the
'deviance' of rationality, such as in ironical and metaphorical sequences, and jokes[23]. (4) The *mood-operator* φ is an important criterion
of classification and diversification. A road indication is clearly a
volitive; an argument, more than a proof, is a volitive; it is an open
and interesting question, in aesthetics and in semiotics, to know

whether art has *one* particular mood (thus, constituting the *essence* of art; is art perhaps a "complex question", a judicative-volitive combination[24] ?) or if various moods, maybe the whole typology of moods, realize in different types of art ('dogmatic' and realistic art is more judicative than abstract art; it without doubt makes sense to state that music, in general, is rather volitive in comparison with painting, in general). Of course, these are speculations. Their aim is suggest that φ is a component of the overall significance, i.e. of what is understood when one is said to understand a work of art. (5) The *propositional content* is evidently an important source of diversification, and I do not want to formulate how a typology could even be started[25]. The truthfunctionality of semiotic sequences is determinable within this p-component of the significance; how the specificity of this truthfunctional part of the significance has to be represented (under the form of *indices* ?) remains, in the frame of this chapter, an open question[26].

I hope it is evident now what is meant when one says that understanding has a non-propositional component. Indeed, the π- and φ- components of the significance are non-propositional but 'psycho-logical' (not in the reductionistic sense as will be argued for in Section 3 and 4 of this chapter but in a strongly constrained sense). Almost any theory of meaning, put forward as a theory of understanding, admits one or another non-propositional component. This is, of course, true for hermeneutical approaches where intuition, *Einfühlung* and *Uebertragung* are necessary conditions of all understanding. My account, however, is totally distinct from the hermeneutical way of treating interpretation and understanding, because the non-propositional part of the significance is as *structured* and *socially open* as the propositional part. Its derivation by means of practical inference is *rule-governed*, and inferential 'strategies' are classifiable, predictible and verifiable. Neither do I think, on the other hand, that the thesis defended here coincides with other representative views in contemporary analytic philosophy, such as Davidson's, Dummett's, and Grice's. Let me, as a conclusion of this section, mention briefly some decisive differences. Against Dummett[27], I maintain that, even when it is true that to use a language and to move in the generalized linguistic practice is to understand it, this practice cannot be a set of interconnected propositions: to understand a semiotic sequence transcends 'grasping' (and 'knowing') its propositional content[28]. Arguing against Dummett that part of the significance and thus part of understanding is non-propositional, I will have to maintain against Grice's classical version of an intentional theory of meaning[29] that the non-propositional part of the significance is *socially open*. S's intentionality, according to Grice, is marked by the fact that S has the intention that his intention *be recognized by X*. This, however, is far from what I call the 'social openess' of intentions. When S intends his intention be recognized, there is still no *active* process of X involved, and the recognition by X need not even be realized, S's intention being *sufficient*. 'Socially open' intentionality of S is a type of intentionality where S wants *that X judges* the common desirability of $[\varphi(p)]$. Indeed, there is not significance, in my sense, without active participation of S *and X*, i.e. without judgement, factual or simulated, by X. Lacking active reciprocity and thus intersubjectivity as a necessary condition of the meaning process, Grice's view leads almost inevitably toward psychologism. The non-propositional component, as I tried to show it, *can* be responsible for the 'social openess' of significances and their intersubjective value: this, however, is not the case in a theory, such as Grice's, where understanding is intended by S without any necessity of a judgment on $[\varphi(p)]$'s desirability by X[S]. Finally and fortunately, Davidson's notion of understanding as *radical interpretation*[30] contains a non-propositional factor which makes significance 'socially open', in the sense I suggested. According to his revised thesis[31], radical interpretation is more than T-theoretical grasping of the canonical derivation of meaning as truth; radical interpretation is *charitable* interpretation, which means that one has to presuppose that users of the language *hold* their sentences to be true: to understand

language one has to understand the working of the Principle of Charity
itself. This, evidently, is the non-propositional factor responsible
for the 'social openess' of the semiotic process. One aspect, however,
is missing in Davidson's treatment: the non-propositional component is
presented by Davidson as a purely methodological principle, and, therefore, it is totally *unstructured*. In my opinion, on the contrary, the
non-propositional component of understanding *is structured*, i.e. *what*
we understand *non-propositionally*, namely the π- and φ-component of
the significance, is typologized and definitely determinable within a
psycho-pragmatic theory of significance. These sketchy comments of
alternative views on understanding conclude the sections of my paper
in which I discuss *what* we understand when we speak of understanding
a semiotic sequence.

2.3 How we understand when understanding

But *how* can we understand significances ? After having developed
considerations on the psycho-pragmatic base (and its anthropological
orientation) of understanding, the next step will be epistemological.
This epistemological stage of the argument functions as a constraint
on the psycho-pragmatic stage where significance was explained as a
autonomous and substantial entity. As I said earlier, the danger to be
avoided is psychologism, reductionism and foundationalism: I consider
a psychologistic theory of significance and understanding - so fre-
quent today[32] - no more and no less than an anachronism[33]. Let me call
the current step of my argument the Epistemological Constraint [34]. The
Epistemological Constraint says that there is no understanding of a
significance π[φ(p)] *without descriptive presentation of* π[φ(p)]*in U*
by S. *How* do we understand a significance ? By the fact that a significance - *all* the components of the significance, i.e. π, and φ, and p -
is *descriptively presentified*[35]: descriptive presentation of π[φ(p)]
by S is a *condition* on understanding the significance by S, and this
is the very argument I would like to defend in the remaining part of
this chapter. First, I develop on the notion of 'mode of presentation'

(Section 3), and secondly on the notion of 'descriptive mode of presentation' (Section 4).

It has to be noticed, from the outset, that *modes of presentation*
are not *beliefs*, and that the Epistemological Constraint does not
provoke the deviation of the psycho-pragmatic theory of understanding
toward an *epistemic* theory of understanding[36]. Beliefs are mental
states or events, whereas modes of presentation are *procedures of*
presentification of π, φ, and p without being mental states or events.
In fact, it may also be useful to mention that modes of presentation
are *relations* rather than events and states, so that a mode of presentation has to be interpreted as a under-a-mode-of-presentation-relation; this is mainly why modes of presentation cannot be substantial
beliefs. It is evident that there is an interesting analogy between
the notion of 'mode of presentation' and *Frege's notion of 'sense'*,
but I insist on three main differences which make the analogy, if not
interpreted and clarified, rather hazardous.

A. Frege introduces *sense* strictly in the domain of singular terms
and predicates; a *thought*, then, is the sense of a proposition[37]. Thus,
the mode of presentation of the p-component of the significance is a
Fregean *thought*. It is well-known that the sense-reference distinction,
and the enlargment of the notion of sense from the minimal scope of the
singular term to the maximal scope of the proposition, is aimed at
finding a solution for some *empirical* problems such as identity, synonymy and analyticity. The introduction of 'modes of presentation' in my
framework has a *general theoretical* ambition; anyhow, the mode of presentation of π and φ can hardly be seen as *senses* because the components
π and φ are non-propositional. However, there is no understanding of
them possible without a under-a-mode-of-presentation-relation. As said
earlier, π is correlated with S's *essential* attitude of acceptance,
whereas φ is correlated with his *local* attitude of acceptance: φ modifying p, and π modifying $[\varphi(p)]$, S's acceptance of $\pi[\varphi(p)]$ can coherent-
ly be called S's (essential and local) *propositional attitude*. Thus,
understanding the overall significance necessitates that (1) the propositional content of the sequence U or the p-component be presentified,

(2) the local propositional attitude of S or the φ-component be presentified, and (3) the essential propositional attitude of S or the π-component be presentified. This, definitely, largely transcends the scope of the Fregean notions of *sense* and *thought*: a mode of presentation, on the interpretation that I urge, presentifies not the object of a singular term (as a Fregean *sense* does) nor the object of a proposition (as a Fregean *thought* does) but a *complex value* consisting of a propositional content *and a* (essential/local) *propositional attitude*. This generalization is seen to be required when one tries seriously to account for *how* understanding of a semiotic sequence is possible.

B. Nevertheless, I try to make the most of the notion of sense/thought in Frege in order to make clear how *modes of presentation* function specifically when they presentify the p-component on the one hand, and the π/φ components on the other. We read in the first paragraphs of *Ueber Sinn und Bedeutung*[38] that the notion of *sense* fulfills three functions. The third function, that of providing entities to be denoted in non-transparent contexts, is of less importance for my argument. The first function is that of "*containing the mode of presentation*" to the subject S, whereas the second function is that of *determining the referent* associated with the sequence. This second function may be the final and central one in Frege, and this is a point where I deviate again from the original Fregean doctrine. Let me call the first function of *sense* the *perspectival function*, and the second one the designative or the '*revealing*' *function*. These two functions cannot be dissociated in Frege and they are, in all cases, complementary. I propose, on the contrary, to dissociate the two functions and to declare the perspectival function of sense/thought the central one and the 'revealing' function of sense/thought supplementary. This means simply that modes of presentation presentify *perspectivally* in U *all* components of the significance: what exactly is presentified are "perspectives" on the value ACC(v), so that the mode of presentation in U is, in principle, 'fragmentary' with regard to the completeness of the

CONTEXTS OF UNDERSTANDING

object and 'infinitely open' with regard to its determinacy. To have a
presentation of ACC(v) is not sufficient to identify ACC(v) *as
an object* (as a referent), but the identification of ACC(v) *as an object* is too strong a requirement for having a significance *presentified*
in U. The minimal and sufficient condition for the presentification of
a significance in U is that "perspectives" on the value AVV(v) realize
in U. The supplementary function of 'revealing' the object (or the
referent) becomes necessary once there IS an object, i.e. once the
propositional content has to be presentified. Thus going back to the
π[φ(p)]-structure of the significance, we can conclude that the π- and
φ-components of the significance or the essential/local *propositional
attitude* of S have to be *perspectivally* presentified in order to be
understood by S and X, whereas the p-component of the significance or
the *propositional content* of U has to be *'revealed' as an object* in its
mode of presentation in S and X in order to be *understood* by S and X.
The dissociation of the two functions of *sense/thought* leads thus toward the distinction between two types of modes of presentation, the
perspectival mode of presentation as the minimal condition of understanding, applicable when non-propositional components of the significance (the essential/local attitude of S) have to be presentified,
and the *'revealing' mode of presentation* as the maximal condition of
understanding, applicable when the propositional component of the significance (the propositional content of the sequence U) has to be presentified.

C. Modes of presentation have an *internal functional role*. Frege,
again, is the starting point to be transcended. No doubt Frege's stress
on the radical distinction between sense/thought and associated ideas
or internal images arising from memories or sense impressions may be
maintained as an adequate remedy against psychologism and reductionism.
An idea, Frege writes, is *subjective*("one man's idea is not that of
another"), and sense/thoughts are general, public and 'understandable'
by anyone. But modes of presentation, as they are realized internally
in S and X, have a *general* functional role. There are internal *constraints* on the possibility of *presentation*, and these constraints can

be called 'functional', to be distinguished from psychological limitations in the inductive and trivial sense (such as memory limitations,
individual idiosyncrasies). The 'logic of presentation' of significances is a logic of the internal functional role of modes of presentation, and, therefore, it is totally distinct from a psychology of 'associated ideas'. The internal functional role of presentations regu-
lates, among others, the relations between perspectival and revealing
modes of presentation, and, within the realm of perspectival modes of
presentation, the 'logical' equilibrium in S and X between the presentified psychological primitives as combined in the wanting-judging
structure (realized in the π- and φ-components of the significance). Conjunction, disjunction, inplication and other so-called 'logical' operations are functionally constrained. Not everything can be presentified
in S and X, and logical operations (as formulated in classical and
modal symbolic logic) have to be checked for their *capacity of presentation* for S and X when understanding a semiotic sequence containing
them. Conjunction, disjunction and implication conform to the internal
role constraining the 'presentability' for S and X when the modes of
presentation are 'revealing' or concern the propositional content of
the sequence, as is shown by the following examples. The conjoined
significance of $\pi[\varphi(p_1)]$ and $\pi[\varphi(p_2)]$ is identical with the
significance $\pi[\varphi(p_1 \wedge p_2)]$, with judicative sentences such as "It
rains" and "The roof is red"; it is an aspect of the internal functional role of modes of presentation that the significances of sentences
such as "It rains" (p_1) and "The trees are wet" (p_2) are conjoinable
under one and the same judgment of the mood φ: $\pi[\varphi(p_1 \subset p_2)]$ which contains an implication judged itself by S (according to φ), and this
judgment of ($p_1 \subset p_2$) can be *understood* by S and X because the judgment
of an implication is *presentable* according to the internal functional
role of modes of presentation. Fortunately, these considerations are
far away from trivial psychology, but, unfortunately, they are very
elementary: they do not even tackle the problem of constraints, exer-
cized by the internal functional role, on the mode of presentation of
the π- and φ -components and especially of the introduction of logical

operations within these components[39].

If my thesis according to which modes of presentation are *conditions* on understanding is true, causal theories of meaning cannot be candidates for a theory of understanding. Casual theories of meaning (Donnellan, Kripke, Evans, Putnam) deny any relevance to what I call in this paper the *Epistemological Constraint*. Therefore, no issue is opened by causalism, once one looks seriously for a theory of *understanding*. It is true that the New Semanticists do not aim explicitly at formulating a theory of understanding. Causal theories of meaning are theories of the reference, in the first place, of proper names, and derivatively, of non-anaphorical uses of demonstratives, of 'referential' uses of definite descriptions and of natural kinds terms[40]. Moreover, the deep motivation of causal theorists is anti-Fregean, and it is even possible to argue that a causal theory of reference excludes, in principle, the very relevance of a theory of understanding. Causalism ignores the *internal functional role* of modes of presentation. This is why a *causal chain*[41] cannot be declared a mode of presentation. Causal chains will uniquely determine the objects they are causes of, being themselves not specifiable without reference to these objects. This means that no internal relations between modes of presentation are recognized to be *constitutive* as means of reference and as means of understanding S's referring (in the case, for example, of assertions). The Epistemological Constraint, in the sense I gave to this term, is a source of determination which is *internal* and *functional* (structural), and not external-causal and genetic. None of the New Semanticists admit that meaning transcends the truthfunctional domain of singular terms, natural kinds terms and definite descriptions, to become significance (with its propositional and non-propositional components). But this is not the most important incompatibility. The major opposition concerns the relevance and the autonomy of the internal functional role of modes of presentation, hence the relevance of an anthropologically based theory of understanding itself.

2.4 Presentification and describability

The Epistemological Constraints needs further elaboration. Modes of presentation are necessary conditions on understanding, and a distinction between perspectival and revealing modes of presentation is valuable though still insufficient. The notion of *presentation* itself remains unclear until it has been decided *how* presentification of significances by S and X is realized. Presentation explains *how* we understand, but it is still an open issue *how* we presentify significance. Two classical solutions are available. Conceptual-role semantics states that S and X presentify significance by *conceptualization*. However, the conceptual approach of presentation will be banned as non-canonical, and this rejection is motivated by a general critical attitude towards mentalism. The canonical approach of presentation is the one determining presentation as *descriptive*: it is, in fact, *by description* that we presentify significances, and, thus, are able to understand them.

Presentation cannot be purely conceptual, merely presentation in the 'language of thought'[42]. A 'language of thought' is an ideolect, and conceptualists run the risk of not being able to transcend the 'inscrutability' of ideolects. It seems to be impossible to clarify the notion of intersubjective sameness of *conceptual roles*, whereas we are looking here for a canonical notion of presentation explaining the *generality base* of understanding. How can significances be presentified for S and X *as common values* when no factor external to S's or X's mind intervenes ? Of course, the conceptualist has a solution: according to his doctrine, the presentation of significance *as a concept* has a generality base which is *internal* to the mind and where intersubjectivity is not at all constitutive: a conceptualist finds salvation only as a mentalist postulating universal (and innate) internal structures. But mentalism and innatism are too high a philosophical price to pay. The Epistemological Constraint has to liberate the theory of understanding from psychologism by imposing *presentation* as a

condition of understanding. However, the Constraint has a second function: to liberate the theory of understanding from mentalism by imposing *describability* (instead of conceptualization) as a condition
of presentation. And this is exactly the last step to be argued for.

Thus the Epistemological Constraint contains the following Principle:

PRINCIPLE OF DESCRIBABILITY: For any significance $\pi[\varphi(p)]$ and any
subject S /audience X, whenever S or X understands $\pi[\varphi(p)]$, then
it is possible there is some description D, such that D constitutes the exact presentation of $\pi[\varphi(p)]$.

This Principle of Describability consecrates the *virtual express-
ibility* of significances. This can look rather unorthodox, mainly in
connection with the non-propositional components π and φ of the significance. This seems to me the only way to escape psychologism as
well as mentalism. I claim that there is no specific wanting-judging
combination constituting the significance of semiotic sequences if this
combination is not *virtually* expressible by description. Of course,
the significance has not to be *factually expressed* but *virtually expressible*. By generalization, I affirm the provocative thesis that
there ARE no psychological primitives to signify nor to understand
when these primitives are not virtually expressible. Describability
is a condition on presentation, and thus on signifying and understanding. Nothing so far has been said on what counts as a description D.
The Principle of Describability being formulated as a strategy directly and explicitly attacking all kinds of conceptualism, a description
D cannot be but *discursive* (linguistic/semiotic) and *paraphrastic*.
This is totally concordant with the considerations I developed on the
axis from the 'perspectival' mode of presentation to the 'revealing'
mode of presentation (Section 3). In the case of the π- and φ-com-
ponents, no propositional content or *object*, event or state of affairs
has to be 'revealed' but *perspectives* on the essential/local *attitude*
of S/X have to be *presentified*, and this perspectival presentation is

realized exactly by paraphrastic-discursive description. The Principle
of Describability is still upheld, and D constitutes the *exact* presentation of $\pi[\varphi (p)]$ in the case D contains a paraphrastic-discursive component presentifying 'perspectivally' the essential attitude π and the
local attitude φ of S/X. The discursive component of D 'revealing' the
propositional content p or the object, event or state of affairs is maybe less paraphrastic and more straightforward designative. But, again,
I stress the fact that even this distinction concerns the *virtual ex-
pressibility* of the significance and not its factual expression. The
Principle of Descriptibility inaugurates the final phase of the theory
of understanding.

One addendum may be formulated, though it is directly deducible
from the Principle of Describability.

ADDENDUM (to the Principle of Describability): If D constitutes
an exact presentation of $\pi[\varphi (p)]$, then D will contain a category
or a relation interpreting $\pi[\varphi (p)]$ as ACC(v).

It is part of the rationality of the significance that the common desirability (or the S-X desirability) of $\pi[\varphi (p)]$ is judged by X, and
that this is what S wants X to judge (see Section 2). Thus, the presentation by description of this essential rationality-aspect is a condition of understanding. The significance will be presentified *as a
common value* by descriptions containing paraphrastic-discursive categories and relations interpreting $\pi[\varphi (p)]$ as *acceptable* for the wanting-
judging structure ('essential', on the level of π , and 'local' on the
level of φ) of both S *and* X. A taxonomy of these paraphrastic-discursive categories and relations able to presentify the common engagement
of S and X in the significance, should be worked out in detail. Index-
ical occurrences of *I, here, now, you, we* and demonstratives in general,
will be of prime importance here, but other paraphrastic-discursive
techniques are surely available. Descriptions of the p-component will
be dependent on the availability of techniques designating 'dialogic-
ally' a truthfunctional domain because here too the propositional content has to be presentified as a *common* value[43]. Presentations of prop-

ositional attitudes are surely more complex, and involve a great deal
of paraphrase. Unfortunately, this taxonomy of paraphrastic-discursive
or descriptive *means* capable of presentifying a significance as a value
of common desirability, is evidently not available. Its sophistication
is a challenge for empirical research supporting the theory of understanding.

This concludes my considerations on the bare framework within
which a theory of understanding can acquire some plausibility and coherence. Objections can easily be raised. Logistic (or formalistic)
oriented philosophers will object to the psycho-pragmatic base of the
theory (Section 1 and 2), whereas psychologistic (or mentalistic oriented philosophers will object to all or most of the aspects of the
Epistemological Constraint (Sections 3 and 4). But one objection is,
no doubt, a *standard* objection because it can be directed against almost all theories of understanding, in the hermeneutical as well as in
the analytical tradition. Opponents of my thesis could, of course, object that these proposals are clearly *circular*, and that understanding
in my view presupposes *prior* understanding *ad regressum infinitum*. The
objection, indeed, could run as follows. My account of understanding
would be circular *in two respects*. (a) Understanding is understanding
of a significance. A significance is practically inferred from the
'given' meaning of a pragma-syntactic structure or the semiotic sequence
U. To infer practically a significance presupposes the *understanding*
of U. (b) Presentation is a condition of understanding, and the canonical form of presentation is presentation *by description*. So the availability of a discursive paraphrase is a condition of presentation,
hence of understanding. But you have to *understand* this discursive paraphrase, otherwise it never enables you to understand a significance.

I must confess that this standard objection does not bother me
very much. I reply with quiet conscience that (a) rests on an *ambiguity*
of the term 'understanding': given or immanent meanings as they are reconstructed in a grammar, are not 'understood': they are *known* once the
grammar is internalized. Pragma-syntactic structures *are not to be un-*

derstood, in the sense I gave to this term, but they are *to be known*.
Knowledge and understanding do not have an intrinsic relation (see
Section 2). Understanding by presentation does not presuppose competential knowledge but it presupposes the fundamental and rational desire of the language user to belong to a community. To know grammatical
rules is still not to *understand significances:* the grammatically immanent meaning is the (necessary) starting-point from which significances are practically inferred and thus understood. I reply with an
even quieter conscience that (b) is true and *has* to be true, given the
basic philosophical insight that there is no priviliged domain *outside
of language* ("reality", "mind") *unaffected* by language, and ultimate
salvation from circularity, once understanding linguistic and semiotic
signs is at stake[44]. However, I defend myself against the identification of the fact that understanding (by presentation/description) presupposes prior understanding - a thesis which I indeed hold - with
'hermeneutical circularity'. My account is neither hermeneutical nor
'circular' (in the hermeneutical sense). Understanding is not a hermeneutical relation (intuition, Einfühlung) with the significance, as
I said earlier (Section 2), because the *overall* significance (thus, the
non-propositional components too) is *structured* and *socially open*. Understanding is not an 'interpretative circle' neither, even when the
availability of discursive paraphrasing is a *condition* of understanding.
It is true that one never transcends language or the sign system in the
view on understanding I would like to be accepted. However, once language is not anymore considered naturalistically or purely 'objectivist-
icallly', but anthropologically embedded, understanding is no longer
a *circle* but a *triangle* of which the basic psychological structure of
men, the common values of the community and the conventional features
of semiotic systems are the distinctive and constitutive factors. 'Circular' understanding is solitary, passive and repititive; 'triangular'
understanding is intersubjective, worldly and creative.

3. PERSPECTIVAL UNDERSTANDING

Whereas causal theories of proper names and of meaning -- Putnam's, say, or Kripke's -- together with their related philosophies of language[45], are trying to recover a pre-Fregean semantic innocence, other representative trends today explicitly declare themselves to be neo-Fregean. Yet I am attracted by neither a pre- nor a neo-Fregean style of semantic analysis, but by a *trans*-Fregean approach: going through Frege to end up somewhere quite remote from him. It is difficult to convince empirical scientists (psychologists, linguists) involved in problems of meaning and understanding that travels of the sort I propose have their intrinsic value; social scientists are interested in meaning and understanding themselves rather than in *theories* of meaning and understanding. Philosophers, in contrast, have to worry about the consistency of theories and about their power to generate empirical hypothesis; and this is why a journey from one theory to another, or a reconstructive look at the *derivability* of the theory from another, is never fruitless. The Fregean cornerstone is inescapable, and a trans-Fregean theory of understanding must of necessity be regarded as a 'liberation fight against the father'.

Were I to summarize my proposal in slogans, I would say: A Fregean semantics is indeed the best candidate to ensure communicability and understanding, but the methodological price charged is too high. If it is the case that what you understand is F(p), then a Fregean theory of understanding will be *bipartite* in its dependence on the strongly delimited sub-theories of *sense* and *force*. Although the force/sense distinction *had* to be made as Frege made it, we must now go *through* it

and transcend it, and not by eliminating one or the other pole of the
bipartition, but -- to use a ridiculously easy formulation -- by setting force *within* sense, or by *unifying* the theory of understanding, in
such a way as to avoid the worst dead-end of all, namely *private* or
hidden meanings and the spectre of incommunicability and solipsism so
abhorrent to common sense.

The unpleasant, rhetorical colour of these slogans should disap-
pear once the theses are translated into technical and highly theory-
dependent terms. The substance of this chapter is concerned specifically with the restructuring of the F(p) formula in order to find a way
out of the bipartition (Section 3.3); and then with the formulation of
the constraints what will guarantee the communicability of the unified
formula - and hence with understanding, or at least, understanding as
it can be established as a theoretical construct (Section 3.4). These
form the substance of the chapter. But first, I sketch what I take *for
granted* even before starting my effort to argue in favour of a particular way of unifying and of constraining the F(p) formula. I take for
granted here what is taken for granted in the Frege-Dummett-McDowell
line of thought[46], but not by the Davidsonians and the truth-conditions
account of meaning and understanding, nor by the 'realists' in general.
Moreover, I abstain from the realism/anti-realism debate and from the
inner formal semantic type of discussion (for example, pro- or contra-
possible worlds). I take things for granted simply as far as my likes
are concerned, without arguing over my dislikes. In the first section
of the paper, then, I start by presenting three 'options' or orienta-
tions, made respectable in current discussions on meaning and understanding by sophisticated arguments. First, the theory of language has
to be *heuristically* oriented; then, the theory of understanding is a
pragmatic theory, or a theory of a practical ability; and finally, the
theory of understanding is an *epistemological* theory, or a theory of
certain type of knowledge.

3.1 PROLEGOMENA

3.1.1. *The heuristic orientation of the theory of language*

By this I mean that *understanding* is a constraint on language as
such, or that the notion of understanding is a constraint upon any
analysis of the notion of language, or that understanding is a constraint on meaning-in-language, or that the theory of understanding is
a constraint on the theory of meaning-in-language. This *asymmetry* between meaning and understanding -- at both the object-level and the
level of their theoretical grasp -- is demonstrated clearly in a definition of language such as (I), where a notion of meaning no longer
appears. *'L is a language only if L is understood'* is, no doubt, an
elliptical definition, to be supplemented by its relation to a community P and its members:

(I)   *L is an actual language of P only if the members of P under-
      stand the utterance of sentences of L (as utterances of L).*

While it looks as if it is possible to start an analysis of the
concept of language without semantic concepts, it seems completely impossible to neglect 'anthropological' concepts. I will avoid using the
term 'psychological' concepts, for in fear I wish to distance myself
from psychologism, which I shall do at every step of my argument. Let
me recall two widely accepted outcomes of (I).

A. First, the structure and nature of the *object* of understanding
does not determine *a priori* the nature and the structure of understanding. So to distinguish simply *types* of understanding would be inadequate, because of the fact that there are different types of *objects*
of understanding. (I), indeed, is a thesis extendable to all semiotic
systems and their entities; one understands a painting, road signs,
jokes, attitudes, persons, texts, and expressions of all kinds -- linguistic, cultural -- and in the ultimate extension, words, stories,
body movements and gestures. However, there *is* indeed a limit: the
object of understanding has to be *expressive* and not undimensional.
When we 'understand' a stone, what we understand is, in fact, the mo-

lecular structure of the stone. (To take examples of other natural-
kind terms: when we 'understand' water, what we understand minimally
-- stereotypes excluded -- is H_2O.) The multidimensionality of 'natural'
terms in understanding has as its basis the fact that, as objects of
understanding, these natural kinds have already been manipulated by
an anthropological supplement or by human intervention; in scientific
understanding, one would say that they are necessarily theory-dependent.
To understand *objects* is to understand *signs,* and signs are mediations:
a sign is [an object + its anthropological supplement] and mediates
between this supplement 'object' and the understander. Returning to
actual languages, which exemplify semiotic systems in general, one notices in (I) that in both the antecedent ('only if members *of P* ...')
and the consequent (' ... language *of P'*), anthropological concepts
are mentioned. The *anthropological* foundation of the theory of understanding does not automatically involve a radicalism such as the statement that there is no incorporation of ontological categorization into
the theory of understanding. All we can say at this very elementary
level of analysis is this: Whatever the incorporation of the ontology
may be, the theory of language (and by extension, of semiosis) obtains
its unity from its *heuristic* orientation -- from the fact that language, as shown in (I), is analyzed in terms of understanding. The
picture would be remarkably different if the theory of language were
oriented by semantic concepts and, in this case, unity as well as categorization would be determined by the ontology itself.

     B. The other point connoted by (I) goes back to the asymmetry of
meaning and of understanding. In some Continental philosophy, especially in hermeneutics with its stress on *Einfühlung* and *Übertragung*, there
is a presupposition that meaning is richer, in principle, than what can
be understood -- that meaning transcends understanding *in principle,*
so that the asymmetry works the other way around. Significance-in-the-
world, in this perspective, has a tremendous primacy over man's weak
capacity to understand it. Understanding here is said to be the spon-
taneous intuitive grasp of an ever-transcending significance. The most

provocative side-effect of the hermeneutical approach towards meaning
and understanding is to be found in the *Methodenstreit* within the 'human' or social sciences. Hermeneutical philosophers of science believe
in the inescapability of the 'irrational' view that social sciences
rely on the type of understanding I have just sketched, and which cannot be further analyzed. The positivist view, on the other hand, holds
that the difference between human sciences (or 'soft' sciences) and
natural sciences is a mere consequence of the retarded state of the
former, where 'hermeneutical' understanding (i.e., rich meaning and
weak understanding) prevails. I take no stand in *this* prolix debate
between the hermeneutical and the positivist approaches within the
philosophy of social sciences. I simply note the fact that the *Methodenstreit* can no longer arise once you take (I) for granted, i.e., once
you admit that semiotic systems -- all meaningful or significant phenomena -- are constructed in terms of understanding of them or, as said
earlier, that understanding is conceived of as a constraint on significance.

Another consequence of (I) is that it becomes rather senseless to
make a distinction, within the theory of understanding itself, between
two traditionally separate topics: *what* can we understand versus *how*
we understand. Although this distinction can have some didactic value,
it does not go further; what we understand, or the independent object
of understanding, *versus* how we understand, or the independent method
of understanding, is, within the framework of (I), and abstract and
parasitic intrusion of levels. This, too, is a consequence of the *heuristic* orientation of the theory of semiosis or, in particular, of actual languages. It is thus a consequence of the avoidance of semantic
notions at the level of this first orientation.

3.1.2 *The pragmatic orientation of the theory of understanding*

This must not exceed the neutral 'anthropological' interpretation,
for otherwise it would become a *psychological* thesis. Let me distinguish, then, between two versions of the requirement that the theory
of understanding be pragmatically oriented. According to the 'anthro-

pological' interpretation, to *master* a language means to understand the
language. Understanding is a *practical ability*, presupposing mastery of
procedures; and understanding as a practical ability rests on the fact
that someone who possesses that mastery is able to do something[47]. The
'anthropological' interpretation of the statement that the theory of
understanding must be pragmatically oriented does not go as far as to
consider this practice of understanding as psychologically determined.
Psychological notions are introduced once the procedures have been
directly associated with idiosyncratic types of communicative intentions and with *local* beliefs and desires of *specific* language users.
However, the understander's understanding will not be seen here primarily as an internal psychological process, but as a practical ability
that is a *process of interpretation of contexts*. Understanding is an
extrinsic rather than an intrinsic ability.

(ii)   *The members of P understand utterances of sentences of L*
       only if they interpret the contexts from which these utter-
       ances are generated.

This is a necessary but not a sufficient condition, and terms like
'interpretation' and 'context' remain unanalysed here. (II) is clearly
a strategic definition to save pragmatics from identification with
psychology on the one hand, and with semantics on the other, or to
preserve the specificity of pragmatic notions with regard to semantic
as well as psychological notions. The *practice* of understanding is not
an activity of the inner life on inner-life primitives; it is a practice-in-the-world or *interpretation of contexts* of understanding. The
anthropological foundation of the theory of understanding does not
automatically lead to psychological reductionism. 'Meaning is use' and
'understanding is a practical ability' -- Wittgensteinian slogans --
guarantee first and foremost the *directness* of the understander towards
contexts of understanding rather than towards the immanent construction
of a mental life.

3.1.3. *The epistemological orientation of the theory of understanding*

The practice of understanding rests on *practical knowledge*. The theory of understanding becomes epistemologically oriented once you admit that implicit knowledge has to be ascribed to the understander; the theory of understanding must specify of what that knowledge consists. Two aspects of this epistemological orientation of the theory of understanding are to be mentioned here: (IIIa) states how the understander's *knowledge* can be formulated so as to avoid mentalism as well as strong realism; (IIIb) shows how a *competential* notion of knowledge is more adequate than an epistemic one. But again, I do not argue extensively about these points in the definition of the understander's knowledge. Rather, I take the *anti-realist* interpretation in (IIIa), and the *competential* interpretation in (IIIb), for granted and as the starting point for the restructuring I attempt later in Sections 3.3 and 3.4.

A. Chomsky's linguistic theory, and that part of psycholinguistics related to it, consecrate 'knowledge of language' as the *explanandum* as well as the *explanans* of grammar. What we know when we produce or when we understand language fragments, in this mentalist perspective, is the *inner language*. The inner language is a meta-language in which representations of the extensions (or the intensions, in the framework of an intensional semantics; for the inner language argument behaves neutrally with regard to the extensionalist-intensionalist controversy) of object language predicates are formulated. One cannot therefore understand an object language unless one already *knows* an inner language or a meta-language. When one understands the predicates of the object language, what one in fact 'understands' is the 'language of thought', to use Fodor's terminological variant[48]. Understanding of the meaning of predicates consists of a mapping of words into an inner representational system. Fodor states explicitly that what happens when a person understands a language fragment must be a translation process basically analogous to what happens when a machine 'understands' a sentence in its programming language.

I move on quickly to the strong alternative view, which is in
fact older than Tarski's and Davidson's, and which has existed in
philosophical literature for as long as philosophers have distinguished between the surface form of expressions and their so-called 'logical' form. The theory of language and of understanding -- even in today's renewed realistic versions -- serves in effect to pair expressions with some kind of canonical representation of their *truth conditions*. Thus to represent the logical form of an expression is to
represent the truth condition of the expression in a way that the expression itself fails to do; to understand this expression is then to
understand this representation of its truth condition. Those who accept
this view do so because they believe that understanding an expression
involves at the very least *knowing* what makes the utterance true, and
this in turn involves knowledge of a truth definition for the language.
To put it once again in Tarskian terms, a truth definition is a theory
that pairs each object language sentence S_O with a metalinguistic sentence S_L, such that 'S_O is true is and only if S_L' is itself a true
consequence of the semantic theory. What one *knows* here, in understanding, is the truth definition for the language, and this knowledge
is presupposed by the understanding of the representation of the truth
conditions of the expression.

In the intuitive eyes of the *realist*, an expression is true or
false if there is something extra-semiotic (or extra-linguistic) *by
virtue of which* the expression is true or false. It is by virtue of
reality that expression are true or false, and to understand expressions is *to know truth and falsity conditions*. In the realist picture,
consequently, there is never any problem over the *accessibility* of
these conditions; this is why the realistic position again will have
to be transcended. The fact that the theory of understanding should
be pragmatically oriented urges for a total reconversion away from the
realist position. Dummett argues, indeed, that there is a conflict between the truth conditions approach to understanding and the pragmatic
approach to understanding, i.e., the approach in which understanding is

taken as a practical ability[49], where, as formulated in (II), members
of P are said to understand expressions when they interpret the contexts from which these expressions are generated. The anti-realist
position, then, holds that one's knowledge of the truth/falsity conditions of an expression lies in one's capacity to *recognize* contexts
as contexts for the expression; or, to be exact, lies in the 'interpretation' of contexts.

It becomes clear now that, by putting the *accessibility* of truth/
falsity conditions at the heart of the theory, the anti-realist answer
is in harmony with the epistemological orientation of the theory of
understanding. As a matter of fact, to say that an expression is true
if and only if there is a (true) context for the expression is to say
that, for any expression E, E is true if and only if there i a (true)
context that would provide *conclusive justification* for asserting E.
The root of the controversy between realists and anti-realists (verifi-
cationists, for example) concerns the primacy in the theory of understanding of the *knowability* or *accessibility* of contexts. That understanding is a practical ability (or that the theory of understanding is
pragmatically oriented) forces upon us the non-realist position where
the supposed knowledge enables the understander to interpret contexts
or, in other words, to recognize individuals, states and events as the
(true) context for an expression; so the supposed knowledge cannot
exist except *in the practice of interpretation*. Thus a reformulation
of the device 'for any expression E, E is true if and only if there is
a (true) context for the expression E', related to the community P --
which, actually, is the criterion for justification -- leads us to
(IIIa):

> (IIIa)   *For any expression E, E is acceptable if and only if there
>   is some context of interpretation that would provide con-
>   clusive justification, constituted in P and relevant to
>   the acceptance or rejection of E by a member of P.*

To understand E, then, is to *have access* to the truth of E. The theory
of understanding is epistemologically oriented by virtue of the fact

that the understander's knowledge is constrained by the *knowability* of
the truth value of E. It is evident that in the influential post-
Tarskian theories of truth and meaning, especially Davidson's, there
is no place for epistemological concepts such as *verification, con-
firmation* and *justification*. This is why post-Tarskian accounts of
truth and falsity of natural language expressions are inadequate in
important respects when they are transplanted into the theory of understanding. The problem of the *relevance of a context* to the truth value
of an expression has been desperately neglected by the truth conditions
account of understanding. I take for granted the verificationist argument against the truth conditions account; the current debate between
strong realism and anti-realism, especially with regard to the principle of bivalence, will be passed over altogether in the next sections
of my argument: anti-realism is presupposed by (IIIb), and thus through
all further steps of the reconstruction.

    B. Another specification concerns the nature of the *knowledge* un-
derstanders have when they are said 'to have access' throughout the
process of interpretation to justificatory contexts. Here I make a
distinctions between *substantial* and *formal* knowledge: 'substantial'
knowledge consists of *contents,* whereas 'formal' knowledge, of *strategies*. It could be said that, for the understander who 'has access' to
a justificatory context, to know means that he has background or basic
beliefs that he shares with and within the community P. This would be
substantial knowledge, or knowledge of contents with their particular
semantic colour and their explicit informational character. However,
this is *not* the way an epistemologically oriented theory of understanding has to go, and I hold that the role of beliefs (background, basic
or common beliefs) has been dangerously exaggerated in current discussions on the nature of understanding. The link between *knowledge*
and *belief* is looser than most of the philosophies of mind suggest.
The type of knowledge I would call *formal* or *competential* knowledge
is not affected by specific contents. Formal or competential knowledge
is knowledge of regularities or, to use a more promising term, of

strategies[50]. Paul Ziff, in his publications on understanding[51], insists that the object of understanding is necessarily *structured* -- what one understands is a network of regularities. I would say that what one knows when one understands language fragments are *strategies of justification*. Interpretation, indeed, rests upon the understander's competence, i.e., on his knowledge of common strategies of justification within P. 'Strategy' is used here rather than rule, condition and function; indeed, strategies are not necessarily correlated with the open surface structure of expressions, nor do they have necessarily syntactic counterparts. As they are deeply concealed, they are demonstrable only by an antropologically founded deduction. (IIIa), as a consequence, has to be supplemented by some further amendment concerning the nature of the understander's competence in understanding:

(IIIb)   *The acceptability of E by the interpreting member of P*
         rests upon his competential knowledge of strategies of
         justification.

Theses (I), (II), (IIIa) and (IIIb) are well-known aspects of one and the same alternative option in current discussions on understanding. The view I will defend rests upon three 'pilars': the structure of the understander, the structure of understanding, and the structure of the object of understanding. None of these 'pilars' has autonomy nor primacy. The programme, consequently, cannot be *reductionistic*: no semantic or logical concepts have to be reduced to psychological ones, nor *vice versa*. In later sections I will attempt to make explicit the theoretical consequences of a position of theses (I), (II) and (IIIa) and (IIIb), in order to create the possibility of falsifying them by arguments based on empirical evidence and on methodological consistency. However, the conviction that a battle must be fought against the Fregean theory of meaning and understanding imposes upon me a 'Fregean interlude': the exact place in Frege from which the transcending jump can be made has to be detected.

3.2   FREGEAN INTERLUDE

An orthodox Fregean could accept the heuristic orientation of the theory of language combined with the pragmatic and epistemological orientation of the theory of understanding. One can, indeed, uphold a Fregean conception of *sense* and at the same time still accept one or another version of a heuristically, pragmatically and epistemologically shaped theory of understanding. However, in this case two developments are needed: the theory of understanding would be *bipartite*, consisting of two somewhat distinct subtheories (the subtheory of *sense* and the subtheory of *force*); and the bipartite theory would have to incorporate as its subtheory of sense an *intuitionistic* theory of truth (where no principle of bivalence functions). I turn now to account for some less-exploited aspects of the notion of *sense* in Frege (without any ambitions towards exegetic exhaustiveness), in order to explore whether there is any possibility of preceeding further along Fregean lines. It all hangs on a suggestive (though not always perceived) shift within the notion of sense, and it is crucial to discover what that shift can imply for a more adequate theory of understanding.

I will not discuss here *sense* in its relation to *force* (see 3.3.1) but, rather, sense in its relation to reference. To go 'through' Frege -- to make the trans-Fregean move -- in the first place means to take seriously the starting point, the sense-reference distinction. According to Dummett, Frege has two arguments for making this distinction, although in both arguments *sense* is said to be *knowledge* (thus orienting the theory of understanding epistemologically). I quote Dummett:

> "... it is unintelligible (according to Frege) to attribute to anyone a piece of knowledge of which the whole account is that he knows the reference of a given expression; ... this referent must be given to him in some particular way, and *the way in which it is given* constitutes the sense which he attaches to the expression"[32].

I will call this type of knowledge and sense *idiolectical*: any speaker must attach *some* sense to an expression that he understands. The other argument says more than this:

"... a plausible account of the informational content of a sentence is impossible if the hearer's understanding of the sentence is represented as consisting ... in a bare knowledge of its reference (i.e., knowledge of the reference unmediated by any sense which is attached to the expression)"[53],

and Dummett states himself:

"What it adds to the first argument is just a *ground* for thinking that sense must be *common to different speakers*"[54].

I will call this type of knowledge and sense *common*. (Here I gladly take into account all connotations, from the Scottish to Moore, of the notion of 'common sense'[55], as will be evident in the subsequent sections of this chapter). Again, an exegesis of Frege is of little importance here. The existence of these two slightly different senses of *sense* is enough for one to guess the very place where the transcending jump can be made.

Do mastery of the language and understanding as a practice presuppose *idiolectical* knowledge/sense, or *common* knowledge/sense ? Notice that most of the definitions of sense in Frege (and in Dummett's book on Frege[56]) are related to the demands of the first argument. Take, for example:

"The sense of an expression is ... that part of its meaning which is relevant to the determination of the truth values of sentences in which the expression occurs"[57],

and

"Sense is ... a cognitive notion; it relates to our mastery of language, i.e., to the way in which we set about determining the reference of our words"[58].

The problem is that idiolectical senses are *not* sufficient to explain a speaker's and an understander's mastery of language. Frege admits the difficulty when he writes:

"So long as the reference remains the same, such variations of sense (between different speakers) may be tolerated, although they are to be avoided in the theoretical structure of demonstrative science and ought not to occur in a perfect language"[59].

One has to be aware of the fact that the understanding of natural language fragments requires likely 'common senses': common senses permit
an explanation of how understanding gives a speaker access to something
greater than just his idiolect. Frege's complaint about the behaviour
of sense in natural languages is that it in fact varies according to
idiolects:

> "To every expression belonging to a complete totality of signs,
> there should certainly correspond a *definite* sense; but natural
> languages often do not satisfy this condition, and one must be
> content if the same word has the same sense in the same context"[60].

Frege presumes that he can make a distinction between sense and reference for a natural language in the same way that it can be made for
axiomatizable theories, which are his initial concern. Once a *single*
notion of sense is applied to natural languages, a considerable number
of tensions becomes evident. Frege is aware of these tensions: in *The
Thought* he writes that, if two speakers associate the same word with
completely different senses, each of which determine the word's reference, then "as far as ... (that word) is concerned, ... (they) do
not speak the same language"[61]. This leads in *The Thought* to a quasi-
solipsistic and sceptical doctrine on the meaning of demonstratives,
particularly of 'I'[62].

Idiolectical senses are not necessarily *private* senses. Dummett
suggests that idiolectical senses can emerge from their privacy to
become fully *public*. I hasten to mention two pairs of concepts that
have their own properties: IDIOLECTICAL versus PRIVATE senses, on the
one hand, and PUBLIC versus COMMON senses, on the other. Idiolectical
senses are not necessarily private, and they can be public though, as
I will argue now, never 'common'. Idiolectical senses cease to be private if they fulfill one minimal condition; this is, as Dummett writes:

> "To be able to use a name, or another word, at all, otherwise than
> in the fashion of a recording apparatus, a speaker must know some-
> thing specific about the way its reference is determined, even if
> he does *not* know *everything relevant*"[63].

To know something relevant about the way the reference is determined
is the minimal condition for idiolectical senses not to be private;
as a matter of fact, private 'senses' are a *contradictio in terminis*,
because there is always a minimal mode of identification of referents,
even in the case of proper names. (This is the familiar point contested by causal theories of meaning, especially by Kripke.) What, then,
can it mean to escape the idiolect ? That there is some form of sense
common to different speakers/understanders of the language should not
be ignored. But the Fregean way leads to *public* sense, never to truly
'common' sense. As Dummett writes, public sense is the overlap of idiolects:

> " ... the sense which is attached by any individual to an ex-
> pression is determined by certain features of what *he* knows.
> Hence there is, on Frege's theory, no room for explaining the
> sense which an expression has in some language otherwise than
> as a sense which all, or most individual speakers of the language
> attach to it. Thus, on Frege's theory, the basic notion really is
> that of an *idiolect*, and a language can only be explained as the
> *common overlap of many idiolects*" [64].

Overlap of idiolects, and thus of public senses -- this is the furthest
one can go along Fregean lines. But is this far enough to ensure communicability and understanding as full mastery of the language ?

Something more would seem to be required, even for those cases
where one can rely on 'overlap of idiolects'. How is overlap possible,
and how do understanders *know* that their idiolect overlaps with other
idiolects ? Moreover, how can the understander be said to possess sufficient (i.e., *minimal*) relevant criteria of identification of referents ? My solution goes as follows: There are shared strategies of
justification, and reciprocal assumptions about these strategies of
justification, and these assumptions are common knowledge. But setting
aside the fact that there is *no* possibility for 'common sense' within
the Fregean framework, one could even say that Dummett's insistence on
the tie between so-called idiolectical sense' and 'public sense' is,
in fact, an effect of *Hineininterpretierung* in the spirit of both Wittgenstein and Quine, where meaning, and thus understanding, never tran-

scend use. This limitation on sense by use - with which I am certainly
in full agreement - seems quite un-Fregean in spirit. Presumably, Frege
would have allowed that every aspect of reference, even one not known
nor understood by anyone, is a candidate for sense; in this perspective the theory of language is, indeed, heuristically oriented. The
link Dummett establishes between idiolectical and public sense attrib-
utes to Frege an implicit adherence to the meaning-is-use doctrine:

> "Frege's thesis that sense is *objective* is thus implicitly an
> anticipation (in respect of that aspect of meaning which con-
> stitutes sense) of Wittgenstein's doctrine that meaning is use
> ..."65.

However, Frege characterized the 'domain of what is *objective*, which
is distinct from that of what is actual', as consisting of things having 'a status independent of the judging subject'[66]. This would mean
that not only the notion of *private sense* -- as said earlier -- but
even the notion of *idiolectical* sense (and its link with *public* sense)
is a *contradictio in terminis*. As Frege notes, what matters for the
purposes of communication -- and of language production and understanding -- is that the speakers can convey/understand which particular reference is being talked about. Hence Dummett's insistence on tying sense
to use does not seem to be required by Frege's thesis that sense is
objective.

Why this long interlude on the Fregean theme ? To understand semiotic systems -- natural languages, for example -- is to understand
senses. There are two paradigms of explanation, which are incompatible
in spite of the subtle shift from one to the other paradigm exemplified
by Dummett's trans-Fregean rather than neo-Fregean formulation. Within
the first paradigm, understanding senses equals understanding the *objectivity* of senses, 'revealing' and identifying the ontology 'without
any loss'; the basis of generality then is the structured ontology (objects, events, states of affairs). Within the second paradigm, understanding senses equals understanding the *community* of senses, hence
identifying the ontology 'perspectivally'; the basis of generality here
is the structured directedness of men towards reality and, ultimately,

the generality of anthropological potentialities. Once one moves within the second paradigm, one has to introduce -- as Dummett does --
pairs of notions like *idiolectical* versus *public,* with their correlates
private versus *common.* The avoidance of private senses, the trans-
gression of idiolects, the account of public senses and, in the end,
the idea of 'common sense' as anthropologically based, are effects of
theories constructed within this second paradigm where, indeed, the
problem of the *community* of senses governs all theoretical effort. Theories of understanding will diverge greatly according to the particular
paradigmatical embedding they manifest or, more concretely, according
to whether their central concern is the objectivity of senses or their
community.

It is the second paradigm that I choose to pursue. I use the term
'perspectival understanding' for the type of understanding that is reconstructed by a theory whose paradigmatical concern is the *community
of senses.* This type of understanding should no longer be called 'objective', but rather 'perspectival', because common sense -- and, in
a less dramatic way, public sense -- identifies the object of understanding (hereinafter called 'significance') *perspectivally* , i.e.,
identifies its object without 'revealing' it fully or 'objectivally'.
Now we see that the Fregean interlude was intended to point out and
to evaluate the paradigmatical shape of a theory of *perspectival understanding of significance.*

3.3 $\varphi(p*\cdots)$

What one understands when one understands significance 'perspectivally' is $\pi[\varphi(p*\cdots)]$.   Section 4 treats the nature and the function of the π-operator. But first, the present section concerns $[\varphi(p)]$,
and how $[\varphi(p)]$ relates to F(p),· the meaning reconstructed by the
bipartite theory of understanding (with its subtheories of sense and
of force). Indeed, once the trans-Fregean move has been made, the problem that first springs to mind is that of the relationship between F
and p in a bipartite theory of understanding. It seems to me that, as

long as a theory of understanding is shaped by the requirements arising
from the centrality of the *objectivity* of senses, the relationship between F and p will necessarily be *paratactic:* F(p), then, would be
rather {p, F}. However, the paratactic analysis, I will argue, should
be excluded in any adequate account of the sense-force relation.

3.3.1. *The paratactic analysis of {sense, force}*

Let me recall how the distinction between sense and force, introduced by Frege, has been interpreted by Dummett throughout his work
on the theory of meaning and understanding[67]. Dummett's picture is as
follows. Any theory of meaning and understanding that as its central
notion takes the concept of truth must, by its nature, consist of two
parts. The core of the theory is the theory of *reference* contained in
a shell forming the theory of *sense;* this subtheory of sense will lay
down of what we are to take a speaker/understander's knowledge of the
theory of reference to consist. To the combined theories of reference
and sense is added a supplementary part, the theory of *force*. Dummett
describes circumspectly the task of this supplementary theory as follows:

> "The theory of force will give an account of the various types of
> *conventional significance* which the utterance of a sentence may
> have, that is, the various kinds of linguistic acts which may be
> effected by such an utterance ... Such an account will take the
> truth condition of a sentence *as given:* for each type of lin-
> guistic act, it will present a uniform account of the act of that
> type which may be effected by the utterance of an arbitrary sen-
> tence *whose truth condition is presupposed as known"* 68.

Dummett is explicit on the autonomy of F and p:

> "The understanding of the *force* attached to the sentence, there-
> fore, itself provides a basis for separating the speaker's grounds
> for his utterance from the content of the utterance itself"69,

> "Truth is an objective property of what the speaker says, deter-
> mined *independently* of his knowledge or his grounds for or motives
> in saying it"70,

and

" ... this compels us to make the sharpest possible distinction between the condition for the truth of a sentence and that which entitles a speaker to make an assertion"71.

It is beyond doubt that, in Dummett, conditions on the validity of F and conditions on the truth value of p can never be identified. What is at stake here is the central methodological point on the relationship between sense and force: truth conditions are taken *as given* and presupposed *as known* before they can be connected with a specific force within the practice of language. Setting it in the context of language acquisition, Dummett writes:

"Having mastered the theories of reference and of sense, [the Martian] has a great deal more to learn: he has to be provided with an explicit description of our linguistic practice in terms of our utterances of sentences whose meanings (conceived of *as given* in terms of their truth conditions) are taken *as already known*"72,

and this is how the Martian *understands* the semiotic systems on earth.

The same methodological position is defended by McDowell. He argues that, even when "certification of a theory as a theory of sense requires it to be capable of functioning in the *ascription of propositional acts*"73, it would be a misrepresentation if the notion of a propositional *act* were taken as conceptually *prior* to the notion of sense. No elucidation of the notion of sense is possible in terms of the notion of force, even if it is possible to describe their connection. Such a connection, in any case, would not affect the autonomy of the two subtheories. To make the problem tangible, I quote here McDowell's formulation of the task of the theory of force:

"First, licence the *identification of linguistic actions,* given enough information about them, as performances of propositional acts of specific types (assertion, question, and so on); and second, show how to recover, from a sufficiently full description of an utterance, which may be an utterance of an elliptical or non-indicative sentence, a suitable designation of a suitable *indicative* sentence. The idea is that a theory of sense and a theory of force, *in combination,* should enable one to move, from a sufficiently full description of a speaker's utterance, uninterpreted, to a *description of his performance as a propositional act* of a

specified kind with a specified content, that is, a description
on the pattern of 'He is asserting that p'... where what replaces
'p' is the sentence used on the right-hand side of the theorem
which the theory of sense *entails for that indicative sentence*
which is warranted by the theory of force *as being suitably* related to the utterance"74.

McDowell adds that descriptions of propositional acts will have to meet
not only the requirements *from within*, which has to do with their autonomous sense, but also the requirement *from outside* the bipartite
theory, namely, that they should fit into the wider context of the
speaker's general (linguistic and non-linguistic) behaviour.

The problem with any paratactic analysis of the connected force
and sense of language fragments -- at work in any theory of understanding where the *objectivity* of sense prevails -- is that there is no way
of unifying the requirement *from within* and the requirement *from outside*. These requirements are simply *juxtaposed*, even when defenders of
this type of theory of understanding state programmatically *that* pieces
fit together, *that* there is no reduction from one to another, that one
piece is not *fixed* by another without reciprocal interaction. This is
precisely the point from which an adequate theory of understanding will
have to deviate. As a standard definition of understanding, where sense
and force are paratactically related, consider (A)[75]:

(A)   *To understand sentences s in language L is to understand that*
      s means p; and s means p if and only if there is a truth-
      theory θ such that (a) it is a theorem of θ that s is true
      if and only if p, and (b) the deliverances of that theory
      combine with an acceptable theory of force and with observed
      linguistic and non-linguistic behaviour to licence the as-
      cription of plausible propositional attitudes to speakers of
      L.

It might be that

      "this approach enjoys the advantages of a fully extensional, sys-
      tematic neo-Tarskian truth theory and ... that it captures the
      distinctive intensionality of the notion of meaning through the

connection forged in (b) with propositional attitude ascriptions"
76.

Yet, I would suppose, the victory is apparent: nothing is gained by any
paratactic analysis of the sense-force relation. But before considering
a more adequate reconstruction, one further word on 'ascriptions of
propositional acts' or 'propositional attitudes' in a paratactic analysis of the connected force and sense of language fragments.

It has been said -- and I have quoted McDowell in this respect --
that the subtheory of force has at least two tasks: first, to spot the
mode of utterance of a sentence (or, the kind of speech act performed
upon an occasion of utterance) and secondly, to obtain for any utterance, whatever its mode and its syntax, a suitable *related indicative
sentence*. To label the common element *indicative* in order to account
for the varieties of modes might seem to presume the truth conditions
theory of understanding. *It is* indeed so, even if there is some independent reason for taking the indicative as primary, e.g., the crucial role of the indicative in language acquisition, or the eccentric-
ity of a language without assertions (though note that the latter is
contested by anthropologists, linguists and psycholinguists -- but
that is another matter). Understanding, then, follows the following
procedure. First, there is some utterance, described as 'He uttered
the noises such-and-such' or, more systematically, *'He uttered the
sentence s'*. Then, the theory of force enables us to identify the mode
m of the utterance, *'He m-ed that p'* (for example, 'He is asserting
that p', 'He is asking whether that p'). This identification of m is
possible only by virtue of the fact that the theory of force pairs an
indicative sentence s' with the sentence s; it is the function f that
tells us: f(s) = s'. The Tarskian truth theory (see (A), condition (a))
will yield a T-sentence as its output: "s' is true if and only if p".
Finally, the redescription, 'He m-ed that p', licences the ascription
of propositional attitudes to the speaker: *'He believes (desires) that
p'* (in the case of assertion or of command). This procedure should be
the process of understanding. Let me summarize it in (B):

(B)   *To understand sentence s in language L is to understand
      that s means p; and s means p if and only if there is a
      truth theory* θ *for L such that (a) it is a theorem of* θ
      *that s' is true if and only if p, and (b) the ascription
      of a propositional attitude to the speaker of L is made
      plausible by the redescription of the mode m of the utter-
      ance which is constrained by a function f such that f(s) =
      s'.*

The inescapable weakness of (B) is that the redescription 'He m-ed
that p' is not a *sufficient* condition for the ascription of a propositional attitude to the speaker. Although the redescription makes
the ascription *plausible,* the intelligibility of these ascriptions is
determined by a vast constellation of factors, transcending the very
much local factor of the mode m of the utterance. The intelligibility
of the ascription is determined by the attitudes and psychological
states of the understander himself, and by the interpretation of the
linguistic context and the non-linguistic context, which are independent of the mode of utterance. As now becomes evident, moreover, the
intelligibility of the ascription is dominated by various practical
maxims, such as rationality, and sincerity conditions, as elaborated
in classical speech acts theory. Where, now, the theoretical consistency of the paratactic thesis stating that the ascribed attitude is
also constrained by the mode of the utterance, which is itself a redescription effectuated by the theory of sense. Even were this true,
(A) and (B) would never fulfill the requirements of a definition of
understanding. For, if one proceeds *paratactically* (e.g., with *'sense*
and something *else* constrained by sense *and* by a lot more' !) or by
juxtaposition of subtheories, it can never be possible to thematize
the dominance-relation between the subsystems. To say -- as do defenders of the paratactic analysis -- that all parts of the theory interact
is programmatic and rather unfair. It is equally unfair to evoke a
'hopeless indeterminacy' of understanding in the case where the centrality of the theory of sense is questioned. It is evident that the

paratactic analysis is strongly motivated by the requirement of the
objectivity of sense (more than by the requirement of their *community*).
But, as will be shown in the next sections of this chapter, this does
not imply that alternative theories -- for example, theories whose construction is guided by the requirement of the *community* of sense --
automatically fall into the trap of indeterminacy.

3.3.2.   φ *is neither a mode nor an attitude but rather a mood*

An alternative approach to the paratactic analysis will have to
justify its trans-Fregean status in respect of two points: first, the
nature of F in F(p), and secondly, the nature of the *relationship* between F and p in F(p). F, being in my view a *modifier of p* -- which
excludes a paratactic analysis --,is neither an 'attitude' ascribed
to the speaker (F as a propositional attitude presupposing the dominance of the subtheory of sense), nor a mode as a grammatical category:
F is φ, a *mood*, and moods are psycho-anthropological categories. The
picture the paratactic theory of understanding presents is: s → f(s) =
s' → m → F(p), where → m is a *redescription* and → F an ascription. When
one takes into account theses (I), (II) and (III) -- i.e., the theses
that to understand an expression E is to know (competentially) strategies of justification whereby the *context* from which E is generated
can be *interpreted* -- one abolishes the distinction between *redescription* and *ascription* as epistemologically irrelevant, for redescription
and ascription do not rest on two specific types of competential knowledge. To understand E is to know the significance of E (to know *that*)
and this in turn equals to know *how*, i.e., to know how to redescribe
this significance. The *Principle of (Re)describability*, indeed, is the
cornerstone of the theory of understanding[77]. Once liberated from the
dominance of the subtheory of sense, there is no longer any reason for
making a distinction between *redescription of modes* and *ascription of
attitudes*. In the new picture, p and φ and π are describable, and this
is the fundamental condition of their understanding -- nothing is 'ascribed' from a stable 'objective' ground such as a T-theory of senses.

According to the classical view, it is beliefs and desires that
form the attitudes ascribed from modes to speakers. For example, the
attitude ascribed to the utterer of a fragment in the assertive mode
is a belief -- this is actually an elliptical ascription, because what
is in effect ascribed is a *belief that E is true or false*. Similarly,
what is ascribed to the utterer of a fragment in the mode of a command
is not *a* desire with a contingent content but *the desire that it should
be the case* or that *it should not be the case that p*. In recent speech
acts theory[78] these ascriptions are called psychological state conditions. (In earlier work by Searle they are called 'sincerity conditions'[79].) I would argue against the idea of truth-functional ascriptions, and thus against the idea of truth-functional psychological
state conditions. Yet, to say that beliefs and desires are satisfaction
conditions does not imply that they are truth-functional, as is presupposed by the paratactic analysis of understanding ('there is an object, an event or a state of affairs, *and* S believes/desires it').
Moreover, φ, being an *act*, cannot be a *state*. In order to avoid the
truth-functional and static conception of φ, I prefer to call φ the
mood-operator.

A first reason for replacing *beliefs* by *judgments,* at the level
of the φ-operator, is that beliefs and judgments have a distinctive
relationship with propositional contents, and that the relationship
between a judgment-operator and a propositional content is not *necessarily* a paratactic one, as is the case with a belief-operator[80]. Dummett perspicaciously notices that there is a difference between principles governing the condition by which we *judge* contents to be true
or false, and principles governing the condition by which we *believe*
contents to be true or false[81]. The term *judgment,* in its usual anthropological sense, is well-chosen within the framework of a theory
of the φ-operator, because when we *judge*, there is an element of *choice*
as to whether or not we *accept* a content as true. And this element of
choice is absent in beliefs. Dummett, however, still captivated by the
dominance of the theory of sense, would maintain a more problematic

theory: sense determines whether or not something *is* a ground for accepting a content, independently of whether we decide to treat (or
judge) that ground as sufficiently strong. However, this view to me
seems inadequate, in that it is built upon the *know that–know how* distinction. To put it in epistemological terms, it would look as if *to
entertain* a sense is a *knowing that,* whereas *to judge* a content is a
knowing how: one knows *by means* of judgment. It is precisely this distinction that I want to avoid: to *know* the truth conditions of a content *is*, in fact, to *judge* on what basis a content is true. But this
identification is trans-Fregean rather than Fregean: *what* one understands when one knows a content to be true, in Frege, is never *how* one
might come to know it -- and still less, as Dummett pointed out, what
might lead a person to *judge* a content as true without knowing it. Fortunately, Dummett himself makes a trans-Fregean move by pronouncing the
sharpness of the clear-cut *know that–know how* distinction to be problematic; and, correspondingly, Dummett (correctly) finds little indication in Frege's account "of how the way in which the sense of a sentence is given, connects with the grounds on which we may base a judgment as to its truth"[82].

Yet, in a more radical trans-Fregean move, how can one argue in
favour of a *know that–know how* identification, or, at least, fill the
hiatus between them ? Two post-Fregean procedures are possible: (a) The
first insists that the theory of sense must explain the way in which a
speaker's grasp of truth conditions *is manifested,* or insists that the
theory of sense (a verificationist one, in this case) must explain that
grasping and judging the truth are both determined by one and the same
set of conditions. This is Dummett's approach; to fill the hiatus happens to involve a reformulation of the nature, and expansion of the
scope, of the theory of sense. (b) The alternative procedure is the
reverse of the first. It requires the expansion of the scope of the
theory of *judgment,* which must explain that judging, a faculty embedded in an anthropological base, is determined by a set of conditions
having a subset identical with the set of conditions that determines

grasping the truth. Grasping the truth is manifested in *some*, but *not*
necessarily *all*, judgments, simply because judgments are not representations but acts, as I will argue in the next section (see 3.3.3). It
is, no doubt, unorthodox for a Fregean to start with a *theory of judging* instead of a theory of sense. It is a complete reversal of perspectives, but not the reversal Kantians and neo-Kantians fear. This is
why Peirce and Grice, both neo-Kantians, demonstrate better than anyone else how to realize the trans-Fregean move. Further, in order to
cope with *desires*, the other traditionally ascribed propositional attitude or psychological state, one has to go back to a *theory of wanting*, and for the same reason: desires are no representational states
extrapolated from modalised utterances that are redescriptions of T-
sentences or axioms of the T-theory. This brings us to the edge of the
double-sided theory of judging and wanting, the anthropological primitives whose constellation determines the specific functioning of the
φ-operator.

The φ-operator functions as the *partial* modifier of the radical
p: it indicates the *mood* of the significance. φ is an operator having
partial scope, because it operates on p according to the *local* attitude
of acceptance (or rejection) by the utterer or speaker S. *Partial* is
opposed to *universal*, and *local* is opposed to *essential* (essential
being the characterization of the other operator π, modifying *in glo-
bo* φ(p). The φ-operator indicates the mood, and moods are distinct
from grammatical modes (indicative, imperative, interrogative) as well
as from basic speech acts (assertions, commands, etc.) where the typology is radically dependent on the existence, in surface or in deep
structure, of conventional means (performative verbs, for example).
The typology of moods of semiotic or linguistic sequences, on the contrary, is a matter of specific combinations of the two anthropological
primitives *judging* and *wanting*. Combining aspects of (I), (II) and
(III), a first approximate definition of understanding the partial
significance φ(p) could be:

(IVa)   *To understand E' as a mood-content structure is to under-*
         stand the local acceptability of E', E' being locally ac-
         ceptable if and only if (a) E' is justified by the context
         of interpretation of φ(p), and (b) the justification of E',
         and thus the interpretation of the significance φ(p),
         rests upon a strategy competentially known by the producer
         S and the understander X.

Let me dwell on the nature and the function of φ in determining the
local acceptability of E'. Perhaps I can best proceed by summarizing
Grice's deep insights on this point[83]. Within the theory of understanding, no argumentation, on the grounds of empirical evidence or of theoretical consistency, is possible over the fact that judging and wanting (or willing) are the anthropological primitives. The distinction
between a so-called 'theoretical' faculty *(reinen Vernunft)* and a
'practical faculty' *(praktischen Vernunft)* cannot be supported by using
empirical evidence from, say, the phenomenon of comprehension of semiotic or linguistic fragments itself. It is by a deductive-transcendent-
al argument (in fact, Kant's) that judging and willing are said to be
the two fundamental faculties of human beings. So, this is imposed
axiomatically on the theory of understanding -- although deductive
argumentation is available in transcendental anthropology. From now
on, I shall talk in terms of two species of *acceptance* of E, viz., *J-*
acceptance and *V-acceptance*, or *judging* and *willing* or, in more common
parlance, *thinking (that p)* and *wanting (that p)*. These categories do
not function as categories of a syntactic or semantic theory of a particular -- or even universal -- language; nor is there any reason to
assume that actual sentences in the language contain unambiguous manifestations of their *moods*. The combination of the anthropological
primitives leads us to the following typology, asking into account
that the φ-operator can be a simple, or unsupplemented, differential
(cases A) or a supplemented differential (cases B):

		φ-operator		radical	
		supplement	*differential*		
1	A	-	S judges	p*	Judicative A
	B	S desires that	X judges	p**	Judicative B
2	A	-	X judges	p*	Volitive A
	B	S desires that	X desires	p**	Volitive B
3	A	-	S desires ($\exists\alpha$) X α-judges	p***	Judicative C
	B	S desires ($\exists\alpha$) that	X desires S α-judges	p***	Judicative D
4	A	-	S desires ($\exists\alpha$) X α-desires	p***	Volitive C
	B	S desires ($\exists\alpha$) that	X desires S α-desires	p***	Volitive D

Some remarks on these types of functioning of the φ-operator would be in order here. There are two 'uses' of the non-complex judicative, (1A) and (1B): sometimes one *declares* that p, S's intention being primarily to invoke the understanding in X that *S judges p*; at other times one *tells* the understander that p, in the hope of making *him*, X, judge that p. The understanding, of the sub-mood (A) or (B) does not involve any recognition of a syntactical or morphological device, nor is there any context of interpretation other than the one *redescribed* as the φ-element. The same distinction exists between two uses of the non-complex volitive, (2A) and (2B). The characteristic feature of the volitive mood is that it relates to *desiring that p*. In the sub-mood (2A), the speaker desires p or wills that p, and this is what X understands, while in the other sub-mood (2B), the speaker wishes to reveal to X that S desires that X wills that p. (It is presumed that willing that p has its standard outcome, namely the actualization of p.) To 'understand' the φ-element in all cases (1) and (2) is simply to understand the concatenation of *non-complex* judicative and volitive primitives.

The cases of the *complex* judicatives and volitives C and D constitute a set of partial significances $\varphi(p)$ that roughly correspond to
question-fragments, although the correlation with a grammatical mode,
for example the interrogative, and with the basic speech act of *re-
quest*, is not at all a one-to-one correspondence. (3A) and (3B) as
question-judicatives are cases in which X understands that S wishes
to obtain an asserted *judgment* (by X or S), usually in the reply to
the question; (4A) and (4B) as question-volitives are cases in which
X understands that S wishes to settle a problem about what *X* is to *do*.
The A-cases in (3) and (4) are the 'rhetorical' cases: (3A), for example, is understood as a case in which S might say that he was just
wondering, 'Is he to be trusted ?'; whereas (3B) is a case in which
the same sentence is uttered as an overt inquiry. Similarly, one can
usually tell whether someone who says, 'Shall I accept the invitation ?'
is merely deliberating with himself or is, rather, seeking instruction
from the audience about performing an action.

It should be noted that, although our examples are linguistic
fragments, the typology covers *all* manifestations to be understood.
The concatenation of V-acceptance and J-acceptance in S and/or X, determining the significance $\varphi(p)$, is the (local) context of interpretation of E. Thus, (IVa) can be interestingly specified by (IVb):

> (IVb) *E' is locally J-V acceptable if and only if: (a) E' is
> justified by a significance whose mood is a correctly in-
> terpretable concatenation of judicative and volitive prim-
> itives; and (b) the justification of E', and thus the in-
> terpretation of φ as a partial modifier of p, rests upon
> a strategy competentially known by the producer and the
> understander.*

3.3.3. φ *is not a representation but an act-indicator*

What then is the state of p as it is modified by φ ? Is p, or the
content, a *representatum,* and φ, or the mood, a *representans* ? This
again would bring us automatically into the sphere of paratactic analysis, where the overall meaning of the expression is said to be {p, F},
or the juxtaposition of propositional content (or sense) and force. In
the definition of φ given in the section above (see 3.3.2), one should
notice at least three ways in which p is 'modified'.

(i) In the cases of the Judicative A and the Volitive A, there is
a relationship between an *unsupplemented differential and the radical:*
to understand expressions of that sort is to understand J(p) or V(p),
with J and V functioning as f, where f(p) = p*. These are the non-complex expressions, because they manifest a simple two-place relationship.

(ii) In the cases of the Judicative B and the Volitive B, there
is a relationship between a *supplemented differential and the radical:*
to understand expressions of these types is to understand V[J(p)], or
V[V(p)], with V(J) and V(V) functioning as f', where f'(p) = p**. These
are cases where the content is modified by a complex function f', and
this is a new step towards the opaqueness of the content.

(iii) In all cases C and D,   and p are once more rendered complex. Some *quantification interior* to the φ-operator (in the differential, in the case of the Judicative C and the Volitive C, and in the
supplement, in the case of the Judicative D and the Volitive D): ∃α is
dominated by an initial desire of the producer and is *imposed* on a J-
or V-acceptance feature (acceptance by X in (3A) and (4A), and by S in
(3B) and (4B)).The structure of the anthropological primitives with its
specific concatenation, and the quantification of α at one or another
point of the concatenation, gives us a highly complex function f'',
where f''(α) = p***.

I call the relationship between φ and p a *functional relation.*
The functional approach to the relationship between φ and p prevents
φ from being a *representation:* φ is an *act-indicator.* This aspect of

the theory of understanding is formulated in (IVc):

(IVc)   *E' is justified by a (partial) significance φ(p) if and
        only if a correctly interpreted concatenation of judicative
        and volitive primitives constrains p such that f(p) = p*,
        or f'(p) = p**, or f'' (α) = p***,where f is an unsupple-
        mented differential, f' a supplemented differential, and
        f'' an internally quantified differential.*

According to the *functional* approach to the relationship between φ and
p, φ cannot be a representation or a *representans* of the content p. The
mood φ is, rather, a *presentification*[84] -- to use a neologism with explicit active or dynamic power *(Vergegenwärtigung)*. φ, being an act-
indicator, 'presentifies' a content such as p*, p** or p***. Judgings
and wantings are not *states* directed towards an *a priori given* content.
In classical terminology it is said that judgings and wantings are intentional 'states' (as the principal subset of psychological or mental
states), because they are directed toward a propositional content.
Truth-functional literature claims that beliefs and desires or propositional attitudes have propositions as their representative content.
Searle argued recently[85] that the notion of representation cannot be
redundant in the theory of psychological states, because at best it
indicates that the relationship between a psychological state and its
object or content is an internal one. In any case, this is the wrong
track[86], even if Searle is aware of the fact that by 'internal relation' one does not mean that one term of the relation, say the content,
is a logically necessary condition for the other term, say the psychological state -- the existence of God is not a *logically* necessary
condition for my belief in God. This would be entailment, or a relationship between two ontologically defined terms. By 'internal relation' Searle means something more formal, namely that the specification
of the state requires the specification of the object or the content.
But even this minimal condition leads to a paratactic analysis such as:
There is a specification (let us say a description) of p, *and* S/X
judges p where S/X's judgment is specified in terms of p's specifica-

tion. The unavoidability of the paratactic analysis, if we regard φ
as a representation of a content p, forces upon us the alternative
view where φ is considered to be the presentification of p*, or p** or
p***, or renders 'present' its content. There does not *exist* a content
(neither as an ontological entity nor as a specification or description), because the content is functionally constrained by the dynamics
of the act-indicator φ.

A final remark should clarify the *role of beliefs* at the level of
the φ-operator. I have argued that *judging,* and not *believing*, is the
anthropological primitive. Beliefs can only be representations, and
never *presentifications*. A set of beliefs, as a φ, could never function
as an act-indicator, since it is nothing but a set of representations.
Beliefs do not have a *constitutive* role within the theory of understanding; they *never replace* the anthropological primitives, even when
they accompany them. Beliefs have to be regarded as, for example, idiosyncratic means of *orienting* the intersubjective relationship between
S and X (beliefs held by S about X, and held by X about S; beliefs held
by S about X's beliefs; and beliefs held by X about S's beliefs). Opponents of this view will argue that *judging* presupposes *believing,* and
that understanding the judging-wanting structure or the 'local' attitude of acceptance by S, is in fact, understanding his beliefs. I am
sure that this is mistaken. Beliefs may be a way of *discovering* what
we understand when we understand φ(p), but they are never *what* we understand nor *how* we understand. What and how we understand depends on
anthropological faculties: the relationship of moods to their contents
is functional, i.e., contents are *not a priori given* but *constituted*
under the scope of the act-indicator φ .

3.4.   π[φ(p*···)]

Here, one might raise an objection: that, far from preventing *indeterminacy* and semantic chaos, the theory of understanding of the partial significance of φ(p*···), at the stage we have now reached, actually creates them. When one no longer admits that communication is

ensured by the mediation of the *objectivity* of senses, one has to formulate another criterion of generality to guarantee full communicability and understanding. The significance of $\varphi(p)$ has been said to be
'partial', and the expression of $\varphi(p)$ cannot be but 'locally' acceptable or an E'. The Fregean interlude was meant to suggest that theories
of understanding are paradigmatically shaped according to the stress
they give to either the *objectivity* or the *community* of significance.
Bipartite theories, like the one where meaning is considered to be $\{p,F\}$,
use as their criterion of generality the *objectivity* of p. The theory
of understanding I favour, on the contrary, formulates as its criterion
of generality the *community* of $\varphi(p^{*\cdots})$. Thus, the overall theory of
understanding will have to include an operator with a universal scope,
the π-operator, guaranteeing communicability and understanding, in order to avoid the indeterminacy of partial significances $\varphi(p^{*\cdots})$. The
criterion of generality, as a consequence, will be embodied in the π-
operator, dominating $\varphi(p^{*\cdots})$ *functionally*, i.e., by no means paratactically juxtaposed to partial significances.

To found understanding on the community of the significance -- as
the necessary condition of generality -- is still a vague procedure,
open to various theoretical translations. The stress on the community
of significances still does not have to lead automatically to the introduction of the π-operator within the theory of understanding. I
want first to present two other proposals, which I call 'reductionistic' approaches to the community of significances. These are erronous
solutions, where the requirement of community is not fulfilled by a
functional π-operator but either by p itself -- thus mapping onto pure
isomorphism objectivity and community of significance -- or by φ --
thus transforming community into mere conventionality. Let me now specify how these reductionistic approaches to understanding have built in
the 'community' of meaning as a condition of generality on which understanding is founded.

3.4.1. The reductionistic analysis of the 'community of significance'

It all depends on the way *common knowledge* of the significance is defined. No theory of understanding can avoid the epistemological orientation; the community of significance is always brought back to common knowledge of the conditions of the production and understanding of semiotic expressions. This common knowledge, in the first type of reductionistic explanation, is a community of *beliefs,* and this is how the reductive directionality goes from community to objectivity; whereas, in the second type of reductionistic explanation, common knowledge is knowledge of *conventions,* and, conventionality being the weakest form of generality, it will be difficult to save this type of explanation from indeterminacy and intranslatability. The first type of reductionistic explanation appeals to the *recursive* statement of common knowledge conditions, and the second to the *conventionalistic* statement of common knowledge conditions.

Defenders of the *recursive* statement of common knowledge conditions would never agree with [IIIa] and [IIIb], our formulation of the epistemological shape of the theory of understanding. For they do not argue in terms of *acceptability* nor of *strategies of justification.* Their deep motivation is to link a truth conditions account of meaning to *actual* languages (the 'actual language relation'[87]). Admitting that understanding is epistemologically constrained, the defenders of the recursive theory of common knowledge support the following course: (i) first, generation of a Davidsonian T-sentence or of a T-interpreted language: $\vdash T_L[T(s) \equiv p]$; (ii) secondly, X takes S's utterance u of the sentences s of the language L as *evident* that F(p), the force (or the psychological state) being added paratactically; (iii) thirdly, X *knows* that S takes his utterance as evidence that F(p), because X *knows* that F(p); (iv) fourthly, to 'know' is evidently to 'believe'; anyone in P, in fact, *believes* that anyone else in P has the knowledge/belief that F(p); (v) fifthly, $T_L[T(s) \equiv F(p)]$ *implies* common knowledge/belief in P that when S and X are members of P, and S utters the sentence s, then X takes S's utterance u as evidence that F(p).

How recursivity and 'common knowledge' (actually, common beliefs)
are related, in this type of reductionistic explanation of community of
significance, is formulated in (C):

(C) *For all sentences s and all meanings* $\vdash T_L[T(s) \equiv F(p)]$, *it
will be common knowledge in P that, for all S and X, to take
the utterance u of s as evidence that F(p) implies that it is
common knowledge in P that all members of P expect, if S utters s, that X will take utterance u as evidence that F(p).*

This recursive statement can easily be framed in a way that dispenses
with the population P, and even of its members S and X, because the so-
called 'actual language relation' is nothing bu the very simple operation of *adding* a non-autonomous *belief* to the definition of a T-lan-
guage: s is true in the language of P if and only if the actual language of P is $\{B(p), T_L[T(s) \equiv p]\}$, where B(p) is a non-autonomous
belief that p. The 'community' of sense and its knowledge is reduced
to the 'objectivity' of sense and the reflecting beliefs held by hypothetical members of P.

The second pattern of explanation holds that 'common knowledge'
is knowledge of the *conventions* regulating recognition of intentions,
in particular, of the intention of communicability. Lewis' definition[88]
is frequently used in this framework: a *convention* in P is a regularity
that members of P *mutually know* to obtain, where, indeed, conventionality and common knowledge are directly related. Using *intensional*
terminology -- to remain within the best Fregean tradition -- where
$M_1 \ldots M_n$ are intensions or meanings[89], one could formulate (D):

(D) *For all sentences s, and all S and X in P, there exists common knowledge in P that, for S and X, if L is* $M_1 \ldots M_n$,
*then S utters u only if S's intentions in uttering u are
within the range determined by one of* $\{M_1 \ldots M_n\}$,

The convention, in this case, says that any member of P utters s only
if his utterance *fits* one of the intensions of meanings of the language
L. In other words, the convention is that everyone has the intention to

communicate, i.e., to utter sentences within the range of the 'objective senses'. Even if the link with *objectivity* is not as strong as in
the recursive statement discussed above, because there is an intermediate term between common knowledge and objective senses (namely, the
overall convention of displaying the universal intention of communication), there still is some reductionism from community to objectivity;
this, indeed, is the only way for conventionality to escape indeterminacy and intranslatability. But the main weakness of the position is
that there is no theory of the basis for this conventional behaviour
of members of P. In this respect, then, the conventionalistic approach
is not fully explanatory. In other words, conventionality is a weak,
vulnerable, 'empirical' universal, and this is why the notion does not
have theoretical autonomy.

3.4.2. *The function of the π-operator*

The alternative view to the reductionistic approach of the community of significance -- the Royal Road or, in Kantian terms, the
transcendental foundation of understanding -- gives full autonomy to
the π-operator and full power to its functioning. The π-operator (to
be translated in approximate common sense terms by 'One can reasonably
conclude that ...', 'the reasonable conclusion is that ...') has the
function of indicating that the significance of the sequence E can be
considered to be the conclusion of a valid argument of *practical reasoning* (or the conclusion of a 'practical syllogism'). The π-operator
indicates the general *rationality* of the significance determined by
the fact that the significance of the sequence E is derived through
strategies of justification (or strategies of practical inference)[90].
The thesis of the understanding of $\pi[\varphi(p)]$ should therefore be formulated in terms of the *essential acceptability* of E, as it is done in
(Va):

(Va)   *To understand E as a rationality-mood-content structure is
       to understand the essential acceptability of E, E being es-
       sentially acceptable if and only if E is justified by the
       context of interpretation of* $\pi[\varphi(p)]$ *, and if and only if*

the justification of E, and thus the interpretation of
$\pi[\varphi(p)]$, *is a strategy competentially known by members*
of P.

Essential acceptability, as well as local acceptability (or acceptability at the level of φ-functioning), is realizable only with regard to
the fundamental faculties of judging and wanting. Essential acceptability is *J-V acceptability,* and what is judged/wanted to be acceptable is
$\varphi(p)$, or p dominated by φ, i.e., a correctly interpretable concatenation of judicative and volitive primitives. Definition (Va), therefore,
can be specified as follows:

(Vb)   *E is essentially J-V acceptable if and only if (a) E is*
       justified by a significance the rationality of which is
       a correctly interpretable concatenation of judicative and
       volitive primitives, and (b) the justification of E, and
       thus the interpretation of π *universally modifying* $\varphi(p^{\star\cdots})$,
       rests upon a strategy competentially known by the producer
       S and the understander X.

The fact that $\pi[\varphi(p)]$ can be translated as 'It is rational that
$\varphi(p)$', or 'To understand, the understander has to intend the validity
of the inference from E to $\varphi(p)$', or 'To understand, the understander
has to want $\varphi(p)$ to be judged by S/X'[91], is expressed by definition
(Vc):

(Vc) *E is justified by a (general) significance* $\pi[\varphi(p)]$ *if and*
       only if a correct interpretation of S's intention of the
       validity of the inference of $\varphi(p)$ *on the ground of the com-*
       mon desirability (or S-X desirability) of $\varphi(p^{\star\cdots})$, *con-*
       strains $\varphi(p^{\star\cdots})$ *such that* $f\,[\varphi(p^{\star\cdots}) = \varphi^{\star\cdots}(p^{\star\cdots})]$,
       where f is π .

It should be clear by now that the theory of understanding appeals to
broad anthropological concepts. Moreover, the justification of rationality transcends the limits of the (empirical) description of rationality in discourse and in semiotic behaviour. The theory of understand-

ing may go no further than the explanation of communication and significative intersubjectivity through the workings of the π-operator, thus
avoiding indeterminacy of significance and semantic chaos. Rationality
itself, as a generality condition, cannot be justified within the theory of understanding itself. My philosophical preference would be to
justify rationality *transcendentally*, in Kant's sense, and to consider
rationality as an *imperative* (whereby rationality can never become a
descriptive concept). This evidence differs radically from the classical accounts of rationality: from both the *external* account of rationality as problem-solving reasoning, and its *internal* account as theoretical (and even 'practical') coherence. It is mainly through the bias
of the π-operator that intentionality and constellations of psychological primitives, as explanatory notions for the theory of understanding, point towards the necessity of an *evaluative* concept with ethico-
metaphysical connotation, such as rationality. Fortunately, no one is
obliged to take the risky step beyond the prudent domain traditionally
reserved for the philosophy of language and for the theory of the meaningful and communicative use of language fragments (and, more broadly,
of semiotic sequences).

As a conclusion, a remark on the title of this Chapter: *perspectival* understanding of significance. According to the inchoative theory defended here, understanding cannot but be 'perspectival', never
'objective'. The trans-Fregean move enables us to liberate ourselves
from the fascination in Western philosophy for truth and objectivity
as the essential values of meaningful and communicative significative
behaviour. A theory of understanding that does not allow the reduction
of the *community* of significance to the objectivity of sense is, no
doubt, unfashionable in this era of philosophical logicism. Indeed,
the focus is on the bi-dimensional transparancy relation between semiotic manifestations and the world rather than on the opaque triangle --
men, world, language -- where the signifying/speaking subject brings
in imperatively its ethical roots.

4. CONTEXTUALISM AND TRANSCENDENTALISM
IN THE THEORY OF UNDERSTANDING

The fourth chapter of this monograph is devoted to further clarifications of two fairly controversial aspects of the theory of understanding inchoately developed here. First, it was said that members of
a community understand utterances of sentences of a language only if
they *interpret the contexts* from which these utterances are generated[92]. This thesis was introduced in order to indicate that the ability
of understanding is a practice-in-the-world and not an activity of the
inner life on inner life primitives. As a process of interpretation of
contexts, understanding is an *extrinsic* rather than an intrinsic ability. Thus I should make this 'pragmatic' or contextualistic thesis
more explicit and elucidate how contextualism is a weapon against im-
pending psychologism. Second, it was briefly suggested that understanding the essential *acceptability* of an expression rests upon the describability of the universal π-operator modifying no matter what partial mood-content significance[93]. I carefully avoided all kinds of
philosophical justification of this strongly constraining *universal*
modification of partial significances, and it should be faint-hearted
not to expose my transcendentalist tendency in this justificatory discussion. Indeed, transcendentalism turns out to be a powerful solution
in this essentially epistemological debate on the foundations of understanding and communication, but only a thorough reconstruction of psycho-pragmatic transcendentalism can keep us away from speculation and
unavailing talk.

One will object that the introduction of contextualism and transcendentalism in the theory of understanding undermines, if not destroys, the Wittgensteinian patronage I claimed throughout earlier chapters. This would be true if contextualism and transcendentalism were seen as the strong doctrines Wittgenstein condemned explicitly. Indeed, the role played by *contextualism* in the calculus model of language inherited from Frege, has been subtly dismantled by Wittgenstein, and neo-Fregean contextualism, applied to the theory of understanding amounting to the claim that we understand sentences in virtue of understanding their constituents, should not hold out after a Wittgensteinian therapy. But the contextualism I favor is not co-textualism - it is a frame wherein understanding can be viewed as practical directedness towards the world, i.e. towards a constellation of contexts. Similarly, Wittgenstein is critical of *transcendentalism,* a tempting philosophical misconception according to which fallaciously reified powers are conceived as occult entities mysteriously contained within the possessor of the power[94]. I accept this criticism, but the Kantian transcendentalism escapes this definition. The Kantian coloration of the theory of understanding, if deviant, is not incompatible with Wittgensteinian attainments: it is an amendment rather than exclusive to the central intuitions of the *Philosophical Investigations*.

Thus nothing should be lost from the Wittgensteinian heritage. The general thematics of the *Investigations* turns out to be truly inspiring, especially the criticism of the Augustinian (and, in fact, Fregean) picture theory of language, and the primacy of understanding in the triad meaning-explanation-understanding. Equally important are particular points as the turning down of our inclination to make of understanding a super-concept rather than a family-resemblance concept, the therapy for our tendency to look at understanding as a mental phenomenon, a state, an experience or one or another general category, and the renunciation of the idea of inner accessibility of understanding (by introspection, for instance). This general and particular thematics precisely favors the idea of *context-boundedness* of understanding, as

I see it. Wittgenstein notices that the *circumstances* are the stage-
setting of the language game containing expressions of understanding:
words are *not* a description of the circumstances in which they are
rightly used (produced as well as understood), and the understander is
justified in his understanding (i.e. "understands with right") not by
his experiences or mental states but by the circumstances of the pro-
duction-understanding use of an expression. It is evident that the key
notions of *justification* and of *circumstance of use* should be elucidat-
ed, and a reconstructive effort to realise this clarification should
not be marked *a priori* as anti-Wittgensteinian: indeed, clarification
of the notion of 'circumstance of use' amounts to a *typology of contexts* of understanding (see 4.1.1.).

Wittgenstein's argument points in the direction of equating understanding with an *ability*. 'Ability', indeed, is a concept very much related to that of 'power' and 'potentiality'. And it is here that the
philosophical misconceptions about ability - for instance, misguided
transcendentalism - can come in. It is as wrong, for Wittgenstein, to
reify the ability of understanding as a substantial and mysterious faculty as it is to reduce ability to its exercise or to its vehicle[95].
Understanding is not what actually *stands behind* its manifestation.
Category mistakes are committed either by *any* equation between understanding and some other psychological state or operation, or by *any* i-
dentification of understanding with its manifestations. The delicate
gesture amending Wittgenstein's therapeutic approach to understanding
is to locate the ability of understanding somewhere between the concealed *faculty*, alien to any use and yet a pseudo-mystery, and the ob-
servable and empirically determinable *vehicles* and *manifestations* of
understanding - this is, indeed, the subtle epistemological position
of the transcendentalia of understanding. Thus, even if contextualism
and transcendentalism are explicit targets of Wittgenstein's undermin-
ing, they will function in an altered form as cornerstones of a well-
equilibrated theory of understanding.

4.1. CONTEXTUALISM

The importance of the contextualistic theme is reflected by the
title of this monograph: *Contexts of Understanding*. The notion of 'context' has been used in very many ways in contemporary linguistic theories and for its unexplicitness it has been criticised by various meth-
odologists. And still I want to argue in favor of a Proliferation Principle with regard to relevant contexts of understanding instead of op-
erating with a Parsimony Principle. This apparent imprudence has to do
with the fact that contexts are differently relevant in a theory of
understanding that they are in a theory of meaning: indeed, the proliferation of contexts can be methodologically inacceptable in a theory of
meaning, *not* in a theory of understanding.

4.1.1. *Types of contexts*

Let me first sketch what types of contexts can enter theories of
meaning, taking into account their specific philosophical embedding
(A.), then what they are in theories of language where production and
understanding are equivalent processes with inverted directionality
(B.), and, finally, what they are in a psycho-pragmatic theory of understanding (i.e. a theory of understanding which has asymmetrical primacy
over the theory of language and of meaning-in-language)(C.).

A. Since theories of meaning are not my concern here, I prefer to
be brief on the relevant types of context for them. Two types of context
can be distinguished according to the richness of the meaning relation
discerned[96]. In the case of a *bipolar* theory of meaning (as most variants of formal and linguistic semantics), i.e. a theory where the meaning of an expression is in its relation to the world of objects, events,
states of affairs and, possibly, to qualities and properties of ontological items, the context should be seen as *presupposed context* directly
manifested by semiotic-linguistic entities without any mediation of a
speaker/understander assuming this bipolar relation. On the contrary,
in the case of a *tripolar* theory of meaning (as most variants of linguistic and philosophical pragmatics), i.e. a theory stating the mean-

ing of expressions in terms of their double-sided relation to the world
and to the internal structure of the language user), the context should
be seen as *actional context*, the action of using the language originating in the internal structure of language producers and understanders and directed at *changing* the state of the world and of worldly
fragments. It should be clear that a *presupposed context* is, in fact,
a set of referents, and the theory of meaning, reconstructing this type
of context, a truth theory of meaning, whereas an *actional context* is
a set of recognisable intentions changing the intersubjective pattern
and the societal life, the theory of meaning,   reconstructing this
type of context, being an intention-convention theory of meaning. However, both meaning perspectives, even when they have been depicted as
dramatically opposed in a "Homeric struggle", should be dialectically
related: both are abstractions with some heuristic value, but they have
in common that *context is* relevant to meaning, as opposed to immanent
and context-free grammars and theories of meaning (such as Katz', where
meaning is tautologically present in the dictionary and in some limited
grammatical operations). Once common sense presents itself on the battle field, it should become clear that presupposing and referring are
themselves actions and, *as actions,* contexts of meaning, whereas specific actions are referents and, *as referents,* contexts of meaning. The
theory of meaning, in the future, will have to investigate whether both
types of context can be unified or not; if this could be done, an en-
tirely new theoretical model would be available for empirical semantics.

B. The *informational* approach to linguistic communication offers
us a view of communication as a process whereby a speaker encodes a
message into a signal from which a hearer decodes the message: this informational model of language use is *bi-directional,* in the sense that
production and comprehension involve the same processes but in an opposite order. The information flow from speaker to hearer could be
represented in Chart 1[97], taking into account that speaker's and hearer's meaning are interpreted as intentional, and that the grammatical
encoding/decoding is done by a transformational generative grammar.

SPEAKER   HEARER

Production 4: ────────────────→ Physiological apparatus
 Acoustic signal   (speech recogniser)
        ↑   │
                                       ↓
Physiological apparatus   Comprehension 1:
 (articulation)   *Phones*
        │
Production 3:   Lexicon processor
 Surface structure   │
        ↑   ↓
Lexico-grammatical   Comprehension 2:
 transformations   *Surface structure*
        │
Production 2:   Syntax-Semantics
 Syntactico-semantic deep   │
 structure (sentence meaning)   ↓
        ↑   Comprehension 3:
                                 Syntactico-semantic deep
Syntax-Semantics   *structure* (sentence meaning)
        │   │
Production 1:   Pragmatics (conventions of
 Speaker's meaning   intentional recognition)
    (S's pragmatic intent)   │
        ↑   ↓
Pragmatics (conventions of   Comprehension 4:
 intentional recognition)   *Speaker's meaning*
                                   (S's pragmatic intent)

CHART 1

I want to mention two main criticisms of the informational schema
as a whole. First, the picture *idealises* linguistic communication in
many respects. There is no possibility of representing neither that
there is parallel and simultaneous processing at different levels within
the speaker and hearer separately, nor that the decoding on the level of
comprehension$_4$ does not necessarily have to go through all other stages
of comprehension *and* does not need the total encoding on all four levels of production. Moreover, the speaker is presumed to be speaking
literally, just meaning what he says: neither indirect speech (i.e.
indirectly expressed pragmatic intents) nor ambiguous utterances can
be accounted for by the informational schema of language communication.
Second - and this is the point where I join my concern for contextualism - *no* types of contextual import can be distinguished: the specificity of contexts is not relevant at all, because nothing but the informational properties of these contexts give dynamism to the flow. Of
great importance is the way information provokes new stages of the
overall process; not at all important (and even outside the domain of
interest of information theory) is how contexts provoke information
(or better, how types of contexts provide types of information). This
is why the notion of context, in the informational framework, cannot
be but vague and heuristically unimportant.

C. A purpose of this monograph is to formulate a theory of understanding which is *asymmetrically* central with regard to any theory
of production, thus being the core of a theory of meaning-in-language
(see 3.1.1.). Understanding can be hardly a process symmetrical to
production because understanding is, in the first place, a process of
practical inference (see 2.1.). Moreover, contexts of understanding do
not exist as static and highly finished data, unlike contents in theories of meaning and in bi-directional informational theories of language - contexts are *contextualisations* for and by understanding (see
4.1.2.). Understanding does not rest upon the solid base of given contexts but understanding *constitutes* them - therefore, all 'contexts of
understanding' are, in fact, contextualisations. This, again, is a

Wittgensteinian attainment: language games *make sense*: they make their contexts. Creativity in language is not the creativity of a calculus; Frege's grand strategy and the post-Fregean fascination for the calculus model of language is deeply mistaken according to the *Logical Investigations*[98]. Creativity, on the contrary, has to do with the *ability* of understanding. The idea of a *given context* is an epiphenomenon of the Augustinian-Fregean picture theory of language. The new paradigm centers around the language games approach, and the family-resemblance concept of understanding as an ability is the core of this new paradigm. One should not be afraid of the proliferation of contexts (as we will see in the next section 4.1.2.), the ability of understanding having the creative force of *justificatory contextualisation*.

This compels us to a typology of contextualisation processes rather than to a typology of contexts of understanding. Whenever 'context' is used throughout my argument, I mean 'contextualisation'. But still some preliminary terminological clarifications should be introduced, namely the opposition between CO-TEXT versus CON-TEXT, and then the opposition between INTRINSIC CONTEXT versus EXTRINSIC CONTEXT. My main concern will be with extrinsic contexts, or rather with contextualisations as the proper characteristics of understanding looked at as an extrinsic ability. Going back to the original formula of *acceptance* (see 2.1.), one should repeat the condition which will enable us to present the typology of contextualisation processes. There is an U(tterance) or a semiotic string; *if* U has the meaning M, *then* U has the significance ACC(v): to 'accept' this significance or to infer practically ACC(v) is to understand $\pi[\varphi(p)]$. The meaning M of U has a co-text; the significance ACC(v) has a con-text; π, φ, p all have an extrinsic context, whereas π is the intrinsic context of $\varphi(p)$, and φ the intrinsic context of p. Let me schematise these and other elaborated notions in Chart 2.

CO-TEXT

When S(peaker) utters U, and H(earer) realises it, then H assumes, by the *Principle of Manifestation* (see below), that S meant something

If M,
Then ACC(v).

CO-TEXT
CONTEXT

Intrinsic context	Extrinsic context		Typology of contexts	Criterion of justification	Types of report
	Phenomenal core	Epistemic supplement			
π	π COMMUNAL CONTEXT C(π)	MUTUAL/IDIOSYNCRATIC	Transcendental circumstances		We / I are/am (in) C(π).
Rationality-context of φ(p)		EPISTEMIC-COMMUNAL CONTEXT B(π)		Authenticity	
φ(p)	Community		Presumptions		I / We believe that π
φ(p)	φ EROTETIC CONTEXT C(φ)	EPISTEMIC-EROTETIC CONTEXT B(φ)	Interactional circumstances		I / We intend that C(φ)
Mood-context of p				Contractuality	
	'Common' desirability		Opinions		I / We believe that φ
p	p ALETHIC CONTEXT C(p)	EPISTEMIC-ALETHIC CONTEXT B(p)	Referential circumstances		I / We know that C(p)
	'Common' denotation		Beliefs	Expressivity	I / We believe that p

CHART 2

by U. The determination of the meaning of U is not part of the process
of practical inference: the meaning of U is the antecedent of the conditional, and it is from M of U that the significance is practically
inferred. However, the working of the Principle of Manifestation, i.e.
that S meant U to express a content M, is evidently an aspect of the
general rationality governing linguistic communication. We should carefully distinguish between three steps: (1) S utters U; (2a) U means M;
(2b) on the basis of hearing S uttering U, H assumes that S means M by
U; (3) *if* S means M by U, *then* H understands $\pi[\varphi(p)]$. I am only concerned here with step (2a), and with the impact of the *co-text* on its
realisation.

It must be presupposed that S and H can rely on their knowledge
of the language. I do not see advantage here in discussing the nature
either of the language as a preformed system or of its knowledge (this
is what grammarians and psycholinguists are supposed to do). The co-
text intervenes when utterances are *grammatically* ambiguous (homonymy,
synonymy, on the lexical level, but ambiguities of a phonological and
syntactical nature as well). Disambiguation can be required and is
usually achieved with the aid of the co-text. Utterances and fragments
of utterances are never isolated in discursive syntagmatics: the co-
text is the 'surrounding text', whatever its extension may be and whatever the discursive units constituting it may be. The co-text has a
(macro)-grammatical structure, and its impact is fairly limited: evidently not all ambiguities can be taken away by co-textualisation; contextualisation, through the process of inferring $\pi[\varphi(p)]$, will be a
lot more powerful with regard to disambiguation. But it should be clear
that *before* the inference starts, and still within the antecedent sequence of the conditional, *grammatical* co-textualisation shapes in an
important way the meaning M from which the significance will be inferred.

INTRINSIC CONTEXT

Within the significance $\pi[\varphi(p)]$ itself, components with a broader
scope can be said to be the context of components with a less broad

scope: in this sense, φ is the *mood-context* of p, and π the *rationality-context* of φ(p). They are intrinsic contexts because of the fact that they do not appeal to trans-semiotic items either of a psychological or ontological order. Thus the presentation of these types of contexts falls together with the discussion of how the φ- and π-operators modify *functionally*, and not paratactically, their arguments (see 3.3.1. and 3.3.2.).

EXTRINSIC CONTEXT

I should be particularly concerned with extrinsic contexts, i.e. contexts which are trans-semiotic - they are the basis on which significances can be practically inferred, but they are *not* part of the significance itself. As is shown in Chart 2, I distinguish between core contexts and supplementary contexts: the core contexts are *phenomenal* contexts of the three components of the significance π[φ(p)], whereas the supplementary contexts are the *epistemic* contexts of these components (they are belief-contexts, called contextual beliefs as well). I symbolise the opposition between the core and the supplement as follows: C(x) versus B(x)[99]. In an 'ideal' case, the inference of π[φ(p)] can be realised without any contextual belief at all, the core contexts being sufficient in order to make the right inferences. But evidently, in most cases, epistemic contexts *are* directing the inference as well. It is of great methodological importance to distinguish, in the supplement part of the extrinsic contexts, two types of epistemic states: the *mutual* ones which are of prime constitutive power while facultative, and the *idiosyncratic* ones which fall outside of any communicative inference process of the significance when understanding. This leaves us with six types of extrinsic contexts which should be presented briefly (starting from the bottom). The procedure of starting with C(p), passing on to B(p), C(φ), B(φ), B(π) and finally C(π), is purely didactic: the practical inference of π[φ(p)] is oriented the other way around. For instance, it is the contextualisation of π, the community, that shapes the context of p, namely the 'common' denotation. This should become clear by my presentation (last paragraph of this section) of some *inference patterns* through the six types of contextualisation.

C(p)

Making abstraction of any epistemic influence (for instance, of mutual beliefs) and of the communal and erotetic contexts, one could say that the context C of the propositional content p is *its denotation:* the propositional content p is inferred (or determined) by the 'interpretation/grasping' of its denotation. The denotation of p *is the referent* of $\pi[\varphi(p)]$. However, this is an abstraction because of the fact that the referent is necessarily a *common* and *intended* one, and this has as a consequence that C(p) is modified by C(φ) and by C (π). As I wrote earlier, the abstraction I am proposing here, is only didactically justifiable. As an abstraction I could say that the referent (or 'referential circumstances') is the context determining the partial significance p. Understanding this partial significance p is to 'interpret/grasp' (as part of the total practical inference) the meaning M of the sign/utterance U and in particular the devices signaling the referent, such as proper names, pronouns and descriptions. It is well known that the interpretation of C (p), without any help of other contextualisations (either phenomenal or epistemic), is simply impossible for the important class of referentially opaque utterances, and this should be the best proof that C(p) is deeply embedded in *all* other types of contextualisations, just like p is necessarily modified by φ and π within the $\pi[\varphi(p)]$ -structure.

I cannot deal here with the technical problems generated by the various sorts of devices signaling the referent (demonstrative pronouns, definite descriptions, etc.)[100]. Evidently, the denotation of p contains the time and space specifications of the referent and the description under which properties and relations can be predicated. To give an overview of all grammatical categories with their specific *expressive* power with regard to the context of p would be to enter in one of the fairly prolific controversies of contemporary philosophy, stimulated recently by the so-called 'causal' theories of proper names (and, by extension, of meaning). My disagreement with causalists (Kripke and, in a sense, Putnam)[101] does not concern their analysis of the relation between an expression, say a proper name or a natural kind term, and its refer- ential circumstances, but the fact that C(p) is not presented as an abstraction or as dependent on other types of contexts (especially the supplementary epistemic contexts such as B(p)).

B(p)

   Knowledge of C(p) can be favored *or* obscured by *believing p*. The epistemic-alethic context of p will have to be interpreted by the under- stander in order to realise full understanding of the significance $\pi[\varphi(p)]$. Only *mutual* beliefs of p are relevant to the communication process: idiosyncratic beliefs (beliefs which are not recognisable or which are not shared by the speaker and the understander) do not enter in the significance of semiotîc strings. Even in the case of proper names can the epistemic-alethic context be a necessary, though supple- mentary, heuristics enabling the understanding of the partial signif- icance p. This is clear in non-literal uses of proper names, such as in the sentence "He is the Aristotle of the XXth century" and even in "Here comes Aristotle" (speaking of the same person considered to be a great philosopher). It is of main importance that not the truth value of a belief constitutes its force of determining the common denotation of p. It can be that *false* beliefs are more effective for that matter than true beliefs are: this is why relevant contextual beliefs should be mutual rather than true. *Common* false beliefs still can help the determination of the referent of $\pi[\varphi(p)]$: the famous case is the one where beliefs are expressed by definite descriptions which are believed to be false of referents but which best suit the conversational object- ives of the speaker/understander ("The man with a martini is a great artist", where the glass of the man contains water). I do not question that expressions of belief have a truth value and that, from the point of view of psycho-logic, the truth functionality of epistemic opera- tions is of prime concern. But I *do* question that this functionality is of some importance for the theory of understanding. From the point of view of understanding, one should distinguish carefully between *knowing C(p)* and *believing that p*[102], between the phenomenal core and the epistemic supplement: contextual beliefs have to fit the conversational objective (hence they are contextualisations) and the truth value of their expression should be retained 'in brackets'. Therefore contextual beliefs are not Fregean senses - they are strategic positions in the dialogic game verifying and falsifying alethic contexts.

C(φ)

    The partial significance φ(p) is a propositional content functionally modified by a constellation of the psychological primitives of judging and wanting[103]. What, then, is the *context* of this judging-wanting constellation ? As I hope to have indicated convincingly[104], this constellation is steeped in *intentionality*. S intends the judging-wanting basis of his utterance to be recognised. This intention, however, is not necessarily *conventionalised* (i.e. to get recognised, S's intention does not have to be expressed in one or another grammatical-conventional way): it is recognisable on the basis of its context, namely the common desirability. To search for recognition, from the side of the producer of the utterance, means to search for a *justificatory* context for the judging-wanting constellation. One cannot think of another context justifying this constellation but its common desirability. Thus it is easy to make the further step by now: the criterion of justification is *contractuality*. As I wrote earlier[105], in order to escape psychologism and circularity, we should accept a criterion of generality: φ(p) has to be a common value, judged by the speaker S and the understander X to be desirable for the S-X community. A common value is an acceptance value ACC(v), and ACC(v) is truly contractual.

    Therefore the context C(φ) is, through the process of practical inference when understanding, the set of interactional circumstances. The interpretation of C(φ) helps the understander X to infer the interactional force of utterances. I prefer 'interactional' to 'illocutionary' force because of the fact that the force of an utterance by S is

modified, from its source on, *by its understanding.* Here again one
should stress that C(φ) is a contextualisation rather than a context -
understanding *makes* its erotetic context interactionally. My criticism
of most speech acts approaches to the force-determination of semiotic
strings is double: first, the force is seen from the point of view of
production, and *not* of understanding (satisfaction conditions are conditions on production intents and their expression), and second, the
paradigm of illocutionary force is that of *literal* illocutionary force
potential, the deviant cases (indirectness, metaphor, irony, sarcasm)
being related to the literal cases by extra transformations[106]. So the
erotetic context should not be seen in terms of types of expressed attitudes, but in terms of types of interactional circumstances. One
should definitely get rid of the idea that psychological state conditions (the conditions that the speaker should *express* such-or-such an
attitude) are the core speech act conditions. Looked at from the point
of view of progressive disambiguation by interpretation of contexts
(on the level we are concerned with, of the erotetic context), one
should say that interactional circumstances constrain very effectively
the partial significance φ(p) when understanding.

B(φ)

The inference route can make a detour on the φ-level by the fact
of *believing that* φ: if B(φ) *replaces* C(φ), misunderstanding will fol-
low; if B(φ) *is added* to C(φ), it can have either an intensification
function or a fallacy function. This type of contextual beliefs could
be called *opinions,* to be distinguished from presumptions and from
beliefs in the strict sense. Unfortunately, the class of opinions within the epistemic supplement - of which, again, only the *mutual,* not i-
diosynchratic, part is effective - has been overlooked in almost all
Anglo-Saxon philosophies of language. The belief B(φ) or the *opinion*
that φ is such-and-such a constellation of psychological primitives
is a very specific context of understanding, to be distinguished from
intending that C(φ) or that such-and-such a constellation of psychological primitives is commonly desirable. These are very proper con-

texts with different inferential power. The epistemic-erotetic context
is the domain of argumentation, overdetermination and rhetorical coloration. It looks as if the inference route making the epistemic-erotetic
detour is subjected quasi necessarily to fallacious interpretation and
understanding. This is too pessimistic and I have a more constructive
view on the import of mutual opinions on the partial significance $\varphi(p)$.
A systematic theory of obviousness, of saliency, of psycho-pragmatic
intensification and overdetermination is required, and the rhetorics
of persuasion as well as argumentation theory are an effective running
start in this respect. The very interpretation of $B(\varphi)$ as a context to
understand fully the partial significance $\varphi(p)$ becomes unavoidable in
all cases of indirectness and of covert or collateral intentionality,
such as deliberate ambiguity, manipulation and lying[107]: the more covert the intentionality of an utterance is, the stronger the import of
opinions on $\varphi(p)$ in the right (heuristic) or in the wrong (fallacious)
way.

B(π)

     The epistemic-communal context $B(\pi)$, like other types of context
within the epistemic supplement, have either an intensification funct-
tion or a fallacy function with regard to the communal context $C(\pi)$,
the global base for understanding. Mutual communal beliefs or *presump-*
tions are clearly an effective context of understanding, though facultative and potentially fallacious (in the case, for example, where the
practical inference of the significance is based on them as the justificatory context *par excellence* without going back to the phenomenal
core at the π level). In order to identify presumptions, I propose
the following criterion: presumptions are this portion of the epistemic
supplement where *maximalisation of agreement* between language users is
required[108]. This maximalisation is only possible on the ground of the
mutual communal belief that language users are self-consistent or, at
least, *maximalise their self-consistency*.

     Two aspects of this self-consistency should be mentioned: (1) the
sincerity presumption, i.e. the mutual communal belief that, whenever

any member S utters U to another H of the community, S is doing so with some recognisable *knowledge* (on the p level) and some recognisable *intention* (on the φ level); (2) the *uptake* presumption, i.e. the mutual communal belief that, whenever any member S utters U to another member H of the community, H can understand U by the interpretation of the contexts of U. Both presumptions, called in the literature 'communicative beliefs'[109], provide a truly generative basis of communication. These presumptions have been specified, in the classical speech act schema, with regard to types of illocutionary acts under the terms of 'sincerity conditions' and 'essential conditions'. However, there has been serious confusion in many pragmatic theories of understanding between the phenomenal core and the epistemic supplement at the π level: indeed, it is a sufficient condition to *mutually believe* (i.e. to presume) that there is sincerity and uptake in order to have a justificatory (epistemic) context for understanding, whereas one should *be*-rational-in-community (or be-in-communal-context) to have a justificatory (phenomenal) context on the π level. It should be stressed that presumptions are *mutual* contextual beliefs[110], thus that either an insincere attitude or the desire of non-uptake in the speaker/understander are *a priori* obstacles to the justification of a significance by B(π). But this does not automatically *prevent* understanding: the speaker/ understander can be *rational* without being sincere and without wanting uptake, or, at the end, without maximalising his self-consistency. This can look fairly controversial, but the distinction between the communal context and the epistemic-communal context should be made in order to explain all kinds of deviant semiotic behavior which is rational on the one hand, and insincere and/or non-communicative on the other: the liar, to be sure, *is* insincere and non-communicative without being irrational... It should be evident that there is no maximalisation of agreement possible on rationality, and this is not true for sincerity and uptake. Disagreement on the rationality of a semiotic sequence leads to *fragmentation* of the community, whereas disagreement on the sincerity or the desire of uptake can lead to discussing the self-consistency of the speaker/understander and further to its minimalisation or maximalisation. This means simply that there is an authenticity, on the π level, which is different from the *mutually believed* authenticity - this foundational authenticity is that of being-rational-with-the-others.

C(π)

The interpenetration and reciprocity of perspectives of members of a community make it possible that a significance can be practically inferred when understanding. All regularities noticed at the various levels within the core and the supplement of the epistemic context can be interpreted to be socio-psychological, thus empirical *norms*, standards and collective rules. However, the 'regularity' of generating the π-aspect of the significance from $C(\pi)$ is not empirical. The community which is π's context, is not a psycho-social and thus empirical group: it is the 'transcendental' circumstance of the basic rationality of the significance. Therefore, a presentation of $C(\pi)$ should be postponed to section 4.2.1. Indeed, the extrinsic context with the broadest scope, namely $C(\pi)$ or the community, is the transcendental base for all empirical contexts, let them be phenomenal or epistemic.

4.1.2. The Proliferation Principle

To urge for the proliferation of contexts appears to be an uncautious and methodologically unjustified gesture. It is true that a non-explicit idea of context-boundedness serves as a *deus ex machina* in quite a number of linguistic theories of language. It should be emphasized, indeed, that 'context', in the study of meaning and significance, is a theoretical construct: this implies for the linguist (but not necessarily for the philosopher) "that he abstracts from the actual situation and establishes as *contextual* all the factors which, by virtue of their influence upon the participants in the language-event, *systematically* determine the form, the appropriateness or the meaning of utterances"[111]. Indeed, the problem, for linguists, is to explicate a pre-theoretical and intuitive notion of context in a theoretical way. The stress on explicitness of 'context' and 'context-boundedness' is evidently differently colored in philosophy and linguistics: linguists want theories as tools for the systematic investigation of the context-boundedness of phenomena whereas philosophers are more interested in the internal coherence of a theory of contextuality. Whatever it might be, the theme of pro- or anti-context is introduced in philosophy of language as the questioning of the possibility of *literal* meaning, i.e. the meaning an utterance (or better, a sentence) has in the 'zero context' or the 'null context'. Indeed, contextualism and literalism, in both their radical and moderate versions, are alternative positions in a prominent debate of today's linguistic theory. In fact, one cannot see how a linguistic semantics is possible without at least moderate literalism: moderate literalism does not claim "that literal meanings are somewhat complete entities, identical to or capable to determine truth-conditions and significance" but they are "schematic meanings, incomplete entities, specifying conditions, guiding principles and other means through which their 'gaps' might be appropriately filled by contextual information"[112]. Moderate literalism expresses probably the only possibility to have an empirical semantics but, to the philosopher, the idea of literal meaning as the meaning a sentence has independently of any context whatever, appears to be an *abstraction* with heuristic value for empirical science but without internal coherence[113]. This debate is far from innocent, especially once one should start the study of 'deviant' cases of meaningful language production/understanding: literalists base their theories of these cases of the firm ground of *direct literal* strategies; they relate literally-based indirect strategies, direct non-literal strategies and non-literally based indirect strategies to the direct literal strategy by the way of supplementary transformations[114], and this is philosophically unacceptable.

The principal source of this misrepresentation is that contexts are considered to be *stable, given* and *finished* states existing before and behind language use. My conception, on the contrary, is that language use, and foremost understanding, *makes* its context: understanding

contextualises signs and expressions. The dynamism of understanding is
that of contextualisation, and it leads as an unavoidable and healthy
consequence to the *proliferation* of contexts of understanding. I cannot
think of a constraint on the proliferation of contexts of understanding,
except π or   the rationality requirement: indeed, rationality is a
transcendental constraint, a non-descriptive imperative which, in its
formality, admits the broadest proliferation as long as this proardation-
tion concerns the empirical (interactional and referential) circumstances of understanding (see 4.2.1.). I insist on the fact that we
should take seriously the dynamism of contextualisation and the proliferation of contexts of understanding. Evidently, this remains a vague
and intuitive guiding principle unless one can make it clear how contextualisation is realised through the practical inference process of
understanding. I introduce here hints for understanding contextualisation. As I noticed in the preceding section, C(p) is the 'common' *deno-*
tation of $\pi[\varphi(p)]$, and C(φ), its 'common' *desirability*. From the understander's *authentic* position of being-with-the-others in the community, which is the broadest context of his rationality, the contextualisation of $\pi[\varphi(p)]$ will have two aspects: the EROTETISATION of φ,
and the ALETHISATION of p. Instead of considering these terms to be
barbarisms, it will be fruitful to explore the idea behind them. Interactional circumstances and referential circumstances are not pre-given,
they are contextualisations: looking at the type of report, one could
say that my intending that C(φ) or my *intention* that interactional circumstances are the context of equals the *erotetisation* of φ as a constellation of psychological primitives, whereas my knowing that C(p) or
my *knowledge* that referential circumstances are the context of p equals
the *alethisation* of p as a set of referents. I concede that there is
no theory of erotetisation and alethisation available, and I assume
that the fetishistic doctrines dominating philosophical thought, namely
ontologism and psychologism, will prevent the construction of such a
theory for another long time. But the Wittgensteinian idea of understanding *as an ability* gives it some credit. First steps, for instance,
would be to get better insight in the proliferation of interactional

circumstances and intersubjectivally shaped psychological events, and in the dynamism of dialogic referentiation[115].

One final point should be added on the *inference patterns* of understanding. Chart 2 shows that the practical inference when understanding potentially has various ways to go, and can traverse the epistemic supplement or not. The inference of the significance $\pi[\varphi(p)]$ will make use either of the phenomenal core of the extrinsic context (pattern A), or of both the phenomenal core and its epistemic supplement (pattern B), or of the epistemic supplement alone (pattern C). Detours are possible in all directions. The inference pattern C where only presumptions, opinions and beliefs are contextualised, leads to *misunderstanding*. The inference pattern A where π, φ and p are contextualised phenomenally without any import of the epistemic supplement should lead to *full understanding*. The inference pattern B where core as well as supplement have import (in a *va-et-vient* from one to the other) is the interesting case: disambiguation and ambiguation are contradictory moves which can lead to understanding or not. The analysis of these inference patterns and the predication of the final result is of foremost importance for the overall theory of understanding.

4.2. TRANSCENDENTALISM

Transcendentalism has a bad reputation[116], and it is quickly identified with speculativism and lack of empirical sense. It is defended by some philosophers in order to escape other kinds of philosophical diseases such as scepticism, solipsism and relativism. As I honestly confessed, I agree with the condemnation of transcendentalism as it has been formulated, for instance by Wittgenstein. However, Kantian transcendentalism is different - it is modest, in the sense that no powers or faculties have to be ontologised. Transcendentalia here are *epistemological* universals, not metaphysical *dei ex machina*. They are 'epistemological' in the rich double-sided semantics of that term: firstly, transcendentalia are the necessary cornerstones *of a theory* of understanding (they are the conditions of the coherence of any possible theory of the ability of understanding) and secondly, they are the self-reflected condition of one's own understanding itself. The peculiarity of transcendentalia consists precisely in this double-sided value of possibility conditions, on the theoretical meta-level, *and* of self-reflected validity judgements, on the subjective object-level: the set of psycho-pragmatic transcendentalia are constraints on the formation of the theory of understanding as well as a subsystem of internalised pragmatic regularities[117].

4.2.1. *Psycho-pragmatic transcendentalia*

The rationality-operator π is a transcendental imperative: $C(\pi)$ is its phenomenal context, and $B(\pi)$ its epistemic context. $B(\pi)$ or the set of presumptions (of which the *sincerity* presumption and the *uptake* presumption are the constitutive portions) does not generate transcendentalia, the epistemic supplement lacking all phenomenal backing. The communal context $C(\pi)$, on the contrary, is phenomenal, and the interplay between the transcendental π-principle and its phenomenal context, i.e. the community, guarantees precisely the specificity of the *imperatives* (or, to use a fully Kantian term, the maxims) functioning with the broadest scope through the practical inference process of understanding. Before I expand briefly on the particular statute of these imperatives in section 4.2.2., let me first give some content to this set of transcendentalia.

It has been said frequently in earlier sections of this monograph that the π-modification can be translated into: "It is reasonable that ..."; this concerns evidently the π-function as an *intrinsic* context of $\varphi(p)$. The π-operator, in $C(\pi)$ or in its relation to the extrinsic context C, *in casu* the community, is a 'quasi'-ethical principle, to be explicated as an interconnection of three dimensions which, from the side of understanding the significance $\pi[\varphi(p)]$, contains the following generative devices:

Dimension 1: There is no rationality of the significance $\pi[\varphi(p)]$ *without manifested content.* MAXIM: Contextualise $\pi[\varphi(p)]$ such that the manifestation of a content is realised.

Dimension 2: There is no rationality of the significance $\pi[\varphi(p)]$ *without interlocutive relation.* MAXIM: Contextualise $\pi[\varphi(p)]$ such that the cooperation of the interlocutors is realised.

Dimension 3: There is no rationality of the significance $\pi[\varphi(p)]$ *without communicative generality.* MAXIM: Contextualise $\pi[\varphi(p)]$ such that the charity/humanity of communication is realised.

Of course, these principles (manifestation, coordination, cooperation, charity, humanity) should be clearly defined. I did this elsewhere[118], and I cannot elaborate on these definitions here. One example will be sufficient. For instance, the Principle of Humanity says: the pattern of relation between knowledge, belief and desire on the one hand, and their contexts on the other, is general on the basis of the *generality* of the speaker/understander's *internal structure.* To 'accept' principles like those mentioned, is to *accept* the maxims, thus understanding the rationality of a significance. Finally, it should be noticed that the acceptance of the workings of these principles does *not* involve presumptions on sincerity and uptake. In fact, they can *generate* presumptions but they are not dependent on them - they are psycho-pragmatic transcendentalia.

4.2.2. *The Parsimony Principle*

The three maxims mentioned here are translations of the π-principle, which contains the overall imperative: *Be rational.* Acceptance of a significance or understanding, is, in the first place, acceptance of this imperative. My conception of understanding is evidently determined by a transcendental-pragmatic argument. It is transcendental in Kant's sense, because it follows the Kantian method of 'transcendental self-reflection'[119]. However, it deviates from classical Kantianism, in a very radical way, because of the fact that the transcendental argument is made possible by *semiotic behavior:* the intersubjectivity of its validity is constituted by the signitive and public acceptance of significances, thus by production and understanding of semiotic fragments themselves. The conception outlined here, therefore, is transendental-*pragmatic:* though the method *is* Kantian, transcendentalism it-

self is 'constrained' by the signitive process at work in the signif-
icance-understanding circle.

The Parsimony Principle is introduced *against* possible proliferation of transcendental arguments. It functions as Occam's Rasor[120]:
transcendental arguments are not to be multiplied beyond necessity.
This is a regulative principle, which may guide. The transcendental
argument, in my framework, concerns *rationality* and *nothing more*. *Not*
the context - be it phenomenal or epistemic - of rationality is transcendental. I am opposed to a notion of 'transendental community' and
'transcendental pragmatics' (Apel, Habermas). The community is the *phenomenal* context of transcendental rationality: it is an extensive notion (just like 'audience') but even the community in its broadest
scope is still phenomenal. Rationality is not; *Be rational* is an imperative without any descriptive substance, and this cannot be true
neither of its context (the communal as well as the epistemic-communal
contexts) nor of its translation into maxims (manifestation, cooperation, charity/humanity). There is no way of understanding without the
acceptance of the quasi-moral domination of rationality.

FOOTNOTES

1. Cf. Rosenberg (1980).
2. Ziff (1972).
3. Cf. Tugendhat (1976: 19).
4. von Wright (1971) and Apel (1979).
5. Cf. Section 3.1.3.
6. Apel (1980).
7. Apel (1980).
8. Gadamer (1960).
9. McDowell (1980).
10. Steiner (1975).
11. Apel (1980).
12. 'Significance', 'acceptance' and 'presentification' (from the verb *to presentify*) are neologisms meant to have a strategic value within the argument: these notions have the function of distinguishing between my own view of understanding and those of classical-logical and semantical theories of understanding, in which the notions 'meaning', 'acceptability' and 'presentation' are central.

13. This cannot mean that there are no locutor and interlocutor having a specific status in the communicative process. To be sure, on the level of everyday communication, they behave differently the one from the other; and that fact is of great importance for conversational analysis. Nevertheless, it is on the level *of the theory* of communication that *non-directionality* emerges: the theory of communication, according to the non-directional view, functions simultaneously both as a theory of meaning and as a theory of understanding.

14. This idea is by no means new. The entire Austinian tradition favors the idea that language fragments are intentional actions, and it is not at all difficult to find support for the thesis that these intentional actions are governed by the principle of rationality. Ducrot presents illuminating linguistic evidence for the fact that linguistic action is *argumentative,* and he develops a linguistic theory totally concor-

dant with the idea of a *meaning process as practical reasoning* (see, among others, Ducrot (1972)).

15. Kenny (1966) is still the most plausible theory of practical inference, especially in its application to imperative sentences.

16. I develop this point in Parret (1981:Chapter III, forthcoming).

17. H.Paul Grice constructed an overall theory of reasoning exactly on the basis of this distinction in his Immanuel Kant Lectures (1977).

18. This opposition, in fact, is at the base of two types of theories of understanding: the *epistemic* theory of understanding, where understanding is explained in terms of knowledge and belief (in the logical and formal semantic traditions, for example), and the *intentional* theory of understanding I am favoring. Thus, *validity* is not meant to be a *logical* property of the argument: an argument is said to be *valid* once it is desirable as a common value of the community.

19. I made some suggestions on this point in Parret (1976). *Veracity*, for example, can be considered a property converting a semiotic object into a *semiotic value*.

20. H.Paul Grice presented the same typology with the aid of the judicative-volitive opposition (cf. Grice (1977)).

21. That even sentences where the meaning and nothing but the meaning of rigid designators is predicated, have a significance of which the propositional part is embedded in a psycho-pragmatic base, may scandalize causal theorists. However, Putnam's notion of "division of linguistic labor" is not totally incompatible with the approach defended here; analogies are perhaps superficial (cf. Schwartz (1977)).

22. Cf. Grice (1977).

23. Conversational implicatures affect precisely this. Grice introduced this notion in connection with the suspension, the weakening or 'flouting' of some maxims derived from the so-called Principle of Cooperation, which is, in fact, a Principle of Rationality (Grice (1975) and Parret (1976)).

24. Isn't a work of art a *rhetorical question* of which the significance can be thought to be: S wants that X judges that   S wants (   ) that X wants that S −judges "p" ? The −operator is really complex here, but it represents maybe the essence of artistic sequences (Cf. Grice (1977) as well).

25. I conjecture that even the notion of "propositional content" is inadequate. There is *no* autonomous content which can be described separately from the non-propositional parts of the significance. The − and   −operator *modify* the radical p, and, thus, can be considered more adequately as *relations* instead of pure 'additions' to an autonomous p. This is a methodological point on the nature of the − and −operators, and, consequently, on how p itself can be interpreted.

26. A note may be added on the *representation* of the significance $\pi[\varphi(p)]$ in a pragmatic science. The practical inference from U (the immanent meaning of the sequence) to $\pi[\varphi(p)]$ is a derivation realized according to pragmatic STRATEGIES. There are three types of pragmatic *strategies*, each of them responsible for *one* component of the overall significance. (1) The subset of PRINCIPLES (for example, *veracity*, *co-ordination*, *charity*, *humanity*; cf. Parret (1976)) interprets the π-operator; the empirical effects of this subset of strategies are the IMPLICATURES. (2) The subset of CONDITIONS interprets the φ-operator; the empirical effects of this subset of strategies are the BASIC SPEECH ACTS (thus, *speech acts* are the empirical effects of *moods*, and a typology of moods cannot be identified with a typology of speech acts). (3) The subset of FUNCTIONS interprets the radical p; the empirical effects of this subset of strategies are PRESUPPOSITIONS. The notion of presupposition I am favoring is *truth-functional* as well as pragmatic. Thus, in a pragmatic science, the propositional part p of the significance will be investigated as being what is *pragmatically presupposed* (in the technical sense of 'pragmatic presupposition', cf. Stalnaker (1973)) by the sequence U. But, again, there is no space here to explore the problem of *representation* of the significance in pragmatics (this problem concerns the representation not only of the components separately but also of the interrelations between the three different components). See Parret (1977) and (1981a, forthcoming). I may add one more point here. To *infer practically* $\pi[\varphi(p)]$ from U is an action effectuated on the basis of 'pragmatic competence' (or, competential knowledge). There is no (mentalistic) danger of using this term once one admits the Kantian perspective according to which 'knowledge *how*' to signify or to understand is *formal* or has to be *reconstructed* as the *possibility condition* of signifying and understanding. 'Pragmatic competence' or 'pragmatically to know how' is, in fact, the internalization of the system of pragmatic strategies (with its three subsets of Principles, Conditions, and Functions).

27. Dummett (1975; 1976).

28. Even the correction that understanding involves knowing the *assertability conditions* (in Dummett (1976)) is not sufficient. I would agree if Dummett accepted, within his theory of understanding, the necessity of knowing the assertability conditions of the non-propositional components and of the significance as well. This, simply, enlarges the notion of 'assertability conditions' to the one I would like to develop (in Section 2.3) once one looks at *how* we can understand significance, namely by its *mode of presentation*. But this enlargement is not allowed by Dummett's theory of meaning where assertability conditions determine the truth-functionality of sequences, and, thus, are necessarily propositional. So, the essential difference with Dummett's position is that the 'knowledge' of assertability conditions is, according to my thesis, non-propositional knowledge.

29. Grice (1957).

30. Davidson (1973, and later publications).

31. See many articles in Evans and McDowell (1976), on the evolution of Davidson's work, and especially on his revised thesis.

32. Today philosophical psychology ('philosophy of mind') devours the philosophy of language and even the philosophy of logic, in Anglosaxon, especially American philosophy ! Of course, not all 'philosophy of mind' has a reductionistic program, but the danger threatens continuously. Moreover, the Gricean option has been developed by his followers in a reductionistic sense, and even Speech Acts theorists seem to take the same direction.

33. As if Husserl, Frege and Russell never wrote their work with its explicit anti-psychologistic motivation.

34. Schiffer calls it the Frege Constraint (1978:171-206).

35. On the neologisms *to presentify* and *presentification*, see footnote 12.

36. See footnote 18.

37. See especially Frege (1956).

38. Frege (1892).

39. Consider, for example, the more controversial case of volitive sentences (such as orders, and some types of questions where one asks for action, not for information): are the constraints, imposed by the internal functional role, concerning logical operations identical when φ is a judicative or a volitive ? Is, for example, the implication of propositional contents, in orders and volitive questions, *presentable* as it is the case when one has judicative φ's?   One gets a tremendous complexity when one tries to state constraints, emanating from the internal functional role, on the relation between the π- and the φ-components: one cannot want the audience to judge (this is the π-component) everything which is a combination of S/X wanting-judging in the φ-component. Consider the example "I want to learn Italian" and "I judge that I can learn Italian by traveling to Italy". Even when I want the audience to judge these two sentences separately, this does not mean that I want the audience to judge that the combination of these two sentences *implies* "I want to travel to Italy". This implication has to be presentable according to the internal functional role of modes of presentation, otherwise it will never be *understood* by either S or X. Anyway, it becomes clear that a theory of understanding needs *more* than a logic of conjunction, etc. *Factual* constraints emanate from the internal functional role of modes of presentation, and these constraints are anthropologically based.

40. This is stressed by Schwartz (1977:13-15).

41. I do not think that differences of the definition of 'causal chain' in Kripke, Evans and Donnellan (who does not even admit the term) affect my argument against causalism in general. For these differences,

see Schwartz (1977:30-34).

42. Thorough discussion of the conceptualist thesis would require precise arguments against the position of Fodor (1975) and Harman (1973).

43. On 'dialogic reference' see Jacques (1977; 1979).

44. This radically anti-reductionistic option is difficult to defend in traditional analytic philosophy where circularity has always been considered the worst disaster a theory can provoke. Fortunately, recent trends in the philosophy of science (Habermas, Feyerabend) and in the philosophy of language (structuralism, for instance) suggest that (a certain type of) circularity is maybe a core methodological strategy for the development of human/social sciences.

45. See Schwartz (1977) with important papers by K.Donnellan, S.Kripke, H.Putnam, W.V.O.Quine, G.Evans, etc.

46. See Dummett (1975;1976) and McDowell (1976).

47. Dummett (1975:114-115) and (1976:69-70).

48. Fodor (1975).

49. Dummett (1976:87-89).

50. See Parret (1981a, forthcoming). A first sketch of this systemics of strategies is given in Parret (1980;1980a).

51. Ziff (1972).

52. Dummett (1975:124) and (1976:128). I rely heavily on this section on discussions I had with Ronald E.Nusenoff (University of California at Irvine) who provided precious materials on Dummett's Frege-interpretation.

53. Dummett (1976:129).

54. Dummett (1975:126).

55. See Parret (1981b, forthcoming).

56. Dummett (1973).

57. Dummett (1973:89).

58. Dummett (1973:134).

59. Frege (1892).

60. Frege (1892).

61. Frege (1956) in Klemke (1968:518).

62. See Parret (1980b, forthcoming), Evans (1980), and Proust (1980).

63. Dummett (1975:131) and (1976:99 and 488).

64. Dummett (1974:523-524, and 527).

65. Dummett (1976:135).

66. Frege (1893:16).

67. Dummett (1976:72-83).

68. Dummett (1976:74).

69. Dummett (1976:87).

70. Dummett (1976:87).

71. Dummett (1976:88).

72. Dummett (1976:130).

73. McDowell (1976:54).

74. McDowell (1976:44).

75. Definition [A] is M. de Bretton Platts' in Platts (1979:67). I
rely in this paragraph on Platts' formulation of a paratactic theory
of understanding.

76. See footnote 75.

77. See Chapter 2 of this book.

78. Among others, in Searle and Vanderveken (1981, forthcoming).

79. Searle (1969).

80. See, on this point, Platts (1979: especially Chapter IX).

81. Dummett (1976:131-137).

82. Dummett (1976:135).

83. This section's debts to Grice's unpublished work will be obvious.
Paul Grice elaborated on the judging-wanting structure and the typology
of combinations of psychological primitives in Grice (1977). I hope
that I understand the essence of his position in the right way. I used
Grice's fruitful classifications in earlier papers: Parret (1979;1980
a).

84. I elaborate the notion of 'presentification' in Parret (1981c,
forthcoming).

85. Searle (1979) and unpublished papers.

86. See my criticisms in Parret (1981c, forthcoming).

87. See Peacocke (1976:170-172).

88. Lewis (1969:78).

89. See especially Loar (1976:138-161) and Schiffer (1977:28-41).

90. I discuss the specific function of the φ-operator in Chapter 2

of this book.

91. See p. 16-19 of this book.

92. See p. 39-40 of this book.

93. See p. 70-72 of this book.

94. See on this point, Baker and Hacker (1980:610-617).

95. Baker and Hacker (1980:612-614).

96. For more details on this distinction, see Parret (1980:610-617).

97. This schema of stages of information flow is an adaptation of the one found in Bach and Harnish (1979:235). The main difference is that my proposal is symmetrical between the speaker's and hearer's processes whereas this is not the case with the Bach and Harnish proposal.

98. See, for instance, the *Philosophical Investigations*, § 81.

99. C from Context, and B from Belief. I will use 'belief' in two senses: a restricted sense where 'belief' is an epistemic-alethic context, and a large sense where 'belief' is an epistemic context in general.

100. I have been interested mainly in the role demonstratives have in referential contextualisation. See Parret (1980b).

101. See Schwartz (1977:Introduction).

102. Of ultimate philosophical importance is the fascinating analysis of the necessity to make a distinction between *meaning* and *believing* in Rorty (1980:Ch. III to VI).

103. See section 3.3.

104. See p. 17-23.

105. See p.18.

106. The first criticism concerns almost all speech act theories, with the exception of Bach and Harnish (1979), whereas the second criticism concerns precisely Bach and Harnish (1979:Ch. II and IV) and others, but with the exception of Searle (see, for instance, Searle (1980:117-136)).

107. See Parret (1979b).

108. Davidson (1973) formulates a Principle of Charity which is, in fact, a complex principle, not to be identified with what I call a Principle of Charity (see below, and Parret (1976)).

109. See Holdcroft (1980).

110. To recall the classical definition of a 'mutual belief': "a mutual contextual belief figures in the speaker's intention and the hearer's inference in the following way: if p is mutually believed between S and H, then (1) not only do S and H believe p, but (2) each believes that the other takes it into account in his thinking and (3) each, supposing

the other to take p into account, supposes the other to take him to take it into account" (Bach and Harnish, 1979:6).

111. Lyons (1977:572).

112. Dascal (1980) presents the debate in clear and convincing terms.

113. Searle (1980:117-129, and 131-136) develops strong arguments against the literalism position, and Dascal (1980) is mainly discussing Searle's contextualistic view of meaning-in-language.

114. This is done throughout Bach and Harnish (1979: for instance, 77-80).

115. See, for instance, on 'dialogic reference', Jacques (1977; 1979). The morals of Putnam (1979) are very instructive: the theory of reference and the theory of understanding are two separate and autonomous theories. This is a clear and respectable position, but the interesting point would be to state the place of a still hypothetical theory of *referentiation* between the theory of reference and the theory of understanding. However, the notion of referentiation itself is still absent from Putnam's treatment of the reference-understanding relation.

116. See Rorty (1980) whose criticisms are only partly justified.

117. On this double-sided statute of 'transcendental' universals, see Parret (1978:137-138).

118. Parret (1976; 1978).

119. See Apel (1980) developing the same pre-conception but without accepting the *Parsimony Principle*.

120. See Grice (1978:118-119).

REFERENCES

Apel, K.O.
   1979 Die Erklären/Verstehen Kontroverse in transzendental-pragmat-
         ischer Sicht. Frankfurt a.M.: Suhrkamp.

   1980 "Intentions, conventions, and reference to things: Dimensions
         of understanding meaning in hermeneutics and in analytic phil-
         osophy of language. In Parret and Bouveresse (eds.) 1980.

Bach, K. and R.M. Harnish
   1979 Linguistic Communication and Speech Acts. Cambridge. Mass.:
         The MIT Press.

Baker, C.P. and P.M.S. Hacker
   1980 An analytical commentary on the "Philosophical Investigations",
         Vol.1: Wittgenstein - Understanding and Meaning. Oxford: Basil
         Blackwell.

Cole, P. (ed.)
   1978 Syntax and Semantics, Vol. 9: Pragmatics. New York: Academic
         Press.

Cole, P. and J.L. Morgan (eds.)
   1975 Syntax and Semantics, Vol. 3: Speech Acts. New York: Academic
         Press.

Dascal, M.
   1980 "Contextualism". In Parret, Sbisà and Verschueren (eds.) 1980.

Davidson, D.
   1973 "Radical interpretation". Dialectica 27.313-327.

De Gelder, B. (ed.)
   1981 Knowledge and representation. London: Routledge and Kegan Paul
         (forthcoming).

Ducrot, O.
   1972 Dire et ne pas dire. Paris: Hermann.

Dummett, M.
   1973 Frege: Philosophy of language. London: Duckworth.

   1974 "Postscript". Synthese 27. 523-524.

1975   "What is a theory of meaning ?". In Guttenplan (ed.) 1975:97–
        138.

1976   "What is a theory of meaning ? (II)". In Evans and McDowell
        (eds.) 1976:67–137.

Evans, G.
1980   "Understanding demonstratives". In Parret and Bouveress (eds.)
        1980.

Evans, G. and J. McDowell (eds.)
1976   Truth and meaning. Oxford: Clarendon Press.

Fodor, J.A.
1975   The Language of Thought. New York: Crowell.

Frege, G.
1892   "Ueber Sinn und Bedeutung". Zeischrift für Philosophie und
        philosophische Kritik 100.25–50. Translation in English in
        Geach and Black (eds.) 1952.

1893   Grundgesetze der Aritmetik. I. Band. Jena: Verlag Hermann Pohle.

1956   "The thought". Mind 65.289–311. Also in Klemke (ed.) 1968.

Gadamer, H.G.
1960   Wahrheit und Methode. Tübingen: Mohr.

Geach, P.T. and M. Black (eds.),
1952   Translations from the Philosophical Writings of Gottlob Frege.
        Oxford: Basil Blackwell.

Grice, H.P.
1957   "Meaning". The Philosophical Review 66.377–388.

1975   "Logic and conversation". In Cole and Morgan (eds.) 1975:41–55.

1977   Some Aspects of Reason (Immanuel Kant Lectures). (unpublished).

1978   "Further notes on logic and conversation". In Cole (ed.) 1978:
        113–127.

Guttenplan, S. (ed.)
1975   Mind and Language. Oxford: Clarendon Press.

Harman, G.
1973   Thought. Princeton: Princeton University Press.

Holdcroft, D.
1980   "Principles of conversation, speech acts, and radical inter-
        pretation". In Parret and Bouveresse (eds.) 1980.

Holdcroft, D. (ed.)
1977   Language and Logic. Warwick: Warwick University Press.

Jacques, F.
1977   "Les conditions dialogiques de référence". Etudes Philosophiques
        3.267–305.

1979   Dialogiques: Cinq essais sur la logique du dialogue. Paris:
        Presses Universitaires de France.

Kenny, A.J.
1966   "Practical inference". Analysis 26.3-

Klemke, E.D. (ed.)
1968   Essays on Frege. Urbana: Illinois University Press.

Lewis, D.
1969   Convention. Cambridge, Mass.: Harvard University Press.

Loar, B.
1976   "Two theories of meaning". In Evans and McDowell (eds.) 1976:
        138-161.

Lyons, J.
1977   Semantics. Volume 2. Cambridge: Cambridge University Press.

Margalit, A. (ed.)
1979   Meaning and Use. Dordrecht: Reidel.

McDowell, J.
1976   "Truth conditions, bivalence, and verificationism". In Evans
        and McDowell (eds.) 1976:42-66.

1980   "Anti-realism and the epistemology of understanding". In Parret
        and Bouveresse (eds.) 1980.

Parret, H.
1976   "Principes de la déduction pragmatique". Revue Internationale
        de Philosophie 30.486-510.

1977   "Conversational implicatures and conventional implications".
        In Holdcroft (ed.) 1977:175-196.

1978   "A note on pragmatic universals of language". In Seiler (ed.)
        1978:125-140.

1979   "Ce qu'il faut croire et désirer, pour poser une question".
        Langue Française 42.85-93.

1979b   "Eléments d'une analyse philosophique de la manipulation et du
        mensonge". Manuscrito 2.119-152.

1980   "Connaissance et contextualité". In Parret, H. et al, Le lan-
        gage en contexte: Etudes philosophiques et linguistique de
        pragmatique. Amsterdam: John Benjamins 1980:7-190.

1980a   "Les stratégies pragmatiques". Communications 32.250-273.

1980b   "Demonstratives and the I-sayer". In Van der Auwera (ed.) 1980
        (forthcoming).

1981   Langage, Rationalité, Pensée: Sur le problème du parallélisme
        logico-grammatical. Paris: Kliencksieck (forthcoming).

1980a   On Pragmatic Strategies: Toward an Integrated Pragmatics
        (forthcoming).

1981b "Common sense: From certainty to happiness". In van Holthoon and Olson (eds.) 1981 (forthcoming).

1981c "A note on representationalism". In de Gelder (ed.) 1981 (forthcoming).

Parret, H. and J. Bouveresse (eds.)
1980 Meaning and Understanding. Berlin/New York: Walter de Gruyter Verlag.

Parret, H. , M. Sbisà and J. Verschueren (eds.)
1980 Possibilities and Limitations of Pragmatics. Amsterdam: John Benjamins.

Peacocke, C.
1976 "Truth definitions and actual languages". In Evans and McDowell (eds.) 1976: 162-188.

Platts, M. de Bretton
1979 Ways of Meaning: An Introduction to a Philosophy of Language. London: Routledge and Kegan Paul.

Proust, J.
1980 "Sens frégéen et compréhension de la langue". In Parret and Bouveresse (eds.) 1980.

Putnam, H.
1979 "Reference and understanding". In Margalit (ed.) 1979:199-217.

Rorty, R.
1980 Philosophy and the Mirror of Nature. Oxford: Blackwell.

Rosenberg, J.R.
1980 "On understanding the difficulty in understanding understanding". In Parret and Bouveresse (eds.) 1980.

Schiffer, S.
1977 "Naming and knowing". Midwest Studies in Philosophy, Vol. II: Studies in the Philosophy of Language 1977:28-41.

1978 "The basis of reference". Erkenntnis 13.171-206.

Schwartz, S.P.
1977 Naming, Necessity, and Natural Kinds. Ithaca/London: Cornell University Press.

Searle, J.
1969 Speech Acts. Cambridge: Cambridge University Press.

1979 "Intentionality and the use of language". In Margalit (ed.) 1979:181-197.

1980 Expression and Meaning: Studies in the Theory of Speech Acts. Cambridge: Cambridge University Press.

Searle, J. and D. Vander Veken
1981 Foundations of Illocutionary Logic. Cambridge: Cambridge University Press (forthcoming).

Seiler, H. (ed.)
  1978 Language Universals. Tübingen: Günter Narr Verlag.

Stalnaker, R.C.
  1973 "Presuppositions". Journal of Philosophical Logic 2.447-457.

Steiner, G.
  1975 After Babel: Aspects of Language and Translation. Oxford: Ox-
         ford University Press.

Tugendhat, E.
  1976 Vorlesungen zur Einführung in die sprachanalytische Philosophie.
         Frankfurt a.M.: Suhrkamp.

Vander Auwera, J. (ed.)
  1980 Determiners. London: Croom Helm (forthcoming).

Van Holthoon, F. and D.R. Olson (eds.)
  1981 Common Sense: A Focus on the Transparent.(forthcoming).

Wright, G.H. von
  1971 Explanation and Understanding. Ithaca: Cornell University Press.

Ziff, P.
  1972 Understanding Understanding. Ithaca/London: Cornell University
         Press.

n the *PRAGMATICS & BEYOND* series the following monographs have
)een published thus far:

1. *Anca M. Nemoianu:* The Boat's Gonna Leave: A Study of Children
   Learning a Second Language from Conversations with Other Children.
   Amsterdam, 1980. vi, 116 pp. Paperbound.
2. *Michael D. Fortescue:* A Discourse Production Model for 'Twenty
   Questions'.
   Amsterdam, 1980. x, 137 pp. Paperbound.
. *Melvin Joseph Adler:* A Pragmatic Logic for Commands.
   Amsterdam, 1980. viii, 131 pp. Paperbound.
. *Jef Verschueren:* On Speech Act Verbs.
   Amsterdam, 1980. viii, 83 pp. Paperbound.
. *Geoffrey N. Leech:* Explorations in Semantics and Pragmatics.
   Amsterdam, 1980. viii, 133 pp. Paperbound.
. *Herman Parret:* Contexts of Understanding.
   Amsterdam, 1980. viii, 109 pp. Paperbound.
. *Benoît de Cornulier:* Meaning Detachment.
   Amsterdam, 1980. vi, 124 pp. Paperbound.
. *Peter Eglin:* Talk and Taxonomy: A methodological comparison of
   ethnosemantics and ethnomethodology with reference to terms for
   Canadian doctors.
   Amsterdam, 1980. x, 125 pp. Paperbound.

SUBSCRIPTION INFORMATION

1 principle annual subscriptions to the series should be taken, but *prepaid*
rders of individual issues will also be accepted.
ubscription Price: Hfl. 200,– per calendar-year (8 texts of each ca. 100-
30 pp.) + postage.
ıdividual texts: Hfl. 30,– + postage; prepayment required.

PUBLISHED BY

John Benjamins B. V., Publisher
Amsteldijk 44 – P.O.Box 52519 – The Netherlands
1007 HA AMSTERDAM
Telephone: (020) 73 81 56 – Telex 15798